Information Technology for the
Not-for-Profit Sector

Information Technology for the Not-for-Profit Sector

IAN HARRIS and MICHAEL MAINELLI

Published by ICSA Publishing Ltd
16 Park Crescent
London W1B 1AH

© ICSA Publishing Ltd 2001

Designed and typeset in Swift and Bell Gothic by
Paul Barrett Book Production, Cambridge

Printed and bound in Great Britain by
TJ International Ltd, Padstow, Cornwall

British Library Cataloguing in Publication Data

A catalogue record for this book is available from the British Library.

ISBN 1 86072 130 3

Contents

Foreword

'The trouble with IT spending,' said the worried trustee faced
with a further bid for resources for another computer system 'is
that it blossoms like dandelions after a shower of rain'. The anxious charity director could only agree, knowing deep down that
the trustee was probably right, but the director was not sufficiently equipped to be sure he had asked the right questions himself of the IT manager who put forward the proposal in the first
place. If only a simple guide for the confused and anxious had
been available, the decision might not have been different, but at
least all parties to the decision would have had a sense of operating from a degree of insight. At last, such a guide is available – *IT
for the Not-for-Profit Sector*. I know because I have read it. I also know
because I was once that anxious charity director.

The book is simply set out, taking the reader through different
aspects of IT within an organisation, be it large or small, identifying the issues that need to be faced and the questions that should
be asked. More importantly, it is based on extensive practical
experience drawn from Z/Yen's involvement with a range of different organisations. Helpful tables – a typical Harris/Mainelli
trademark I am bound to conclude – provide quick reference
points for the incredibly busy executive and the book is broken
into easily accessible subjects. You won't become a computer
expert by reading this book but it will help you develop a sense of
perspective on the way. You may also find that it provides you
with ideas on how to do more with IT inside your organisation.

By the way, we went ahead with the computer system and it
proved a very effective tool within the organisation – phew!

Ian Theodoreson
Director of Finance and Corporate Services, Barnardo's
February 2001

Preface

Why have we written this book?

The application of information technology (IT) has become a pervasive part of organisational life for not-for-profit organisations
large, medium, small and even tiny. In 1999, ICSA Publishing
realised that its Charities Manual was missing something by not
covering IT. Meanwhile Z/Yen, the authors' risk/reward management practice, had by stealth increased its activities in the not-
for-profit sector, especially IT related work, for some years. Several
members of the Charities Manual's editorial board knew Z/Yen
and in particular the Mainelli and Harris literary double act. ICSA
approached us to add a new chapter. Naturally, we requested a
massive advance but strangely our request was dismissed. Film
rights were the subject of much heated debate. Finally, after photographs of our antics at an especially wild Charity Finance
Directors' Group party were laid on the table, it was a matter of
moments before we were signed as bonded authors.

The response to the IT chapter was very favourable. ICSA
Publishing raised the possibility of a book, building on the material in the manual. Neither author remembers ever attending an
ACEVO rave, but ICSA apparently had photographs so we were
bonded once again. We realised that no one had published a comprehensive book on the application of IT for the not-for-profit
sector and that such a book should exist. So here it is.

Who should read this book?

Anyone involved in a not-for-profit sector organisation who
is interested in ensuring that their organisation benefits
from the use of IT. The not-for-profit sector is diverse. It covers

charities, campaigning organisations, trades unions, membership organisations, grant-making trusts and foundations, educa-
tional establishments, health trusts, friendly societies, religious
orders, housing associations – the list can be extended endlessly.
Your not-for-profit organisation might be large, medium-sized,
small or tiny. You might be a chief executive, director, finance
person, IT person, fundraiser, department manager, administrator, service provider, trustee, volunteer, several of these or just
interested.

You might be a student of not-for-profit management or the
practical application of information technology. You might be an
advisor to not-for-profit organisations.

You might not even be involved in the not-for-profit sector, as
much of the advice in this book would help any organisation, be it
commercial, public sector or not-for-profit. Not-for-profit organisations have certain characteristics that are not always shared by
businesses. For example, not-for-profits tend to be impecunious
(and are always guardians of money intended for others). They
tend to be heavily consultative and thoughtful (sometimes exces-
sively so) before implementing change. Not-for-profits have some
sector-specific systems and procedures (e.g. Gift Aid fundraising
and legacies processing). However, in most aspects of applying IT
for the benefit of the organisation, there is little or no difference
between good practice for a not-for-profit and for any other business or organisation.

We have tried as best we can to make the book as useful as possible to a diverse audience, with an emphasis on not-for-profit
specific examples and issues. Even when we use examples or discuss issues that are not directly relevant to you, we hope the content will at least open your mind to possibilities.

What will readers gain from this book?

Our aim is for this to be both a handy reference book and one
for reading. We anticipate that most readers will dip into the
book when they have particular issues to address or tasks to
perform. We hope that you will find the checklists, templates,
practical tips and examples helpful. However, the book has
also been written to allow the interested reader to spend an
evening or a weekend reflecting upon the use and possible uses of
IT in their organisation. In short, we aim to help the reader to
think and provoke thought about IT and weigh up options for
improvement. Most importantly, though, we aim to provide practical help to enable the reader to achieve the improvements
sought.

Who should not read this book?

Do not read this book:

- If you want to learn masses about the technical aspects of IT – there are plenty of good textbooks on computers, computing and 'computer science'. We have tried to minimise (but not eliminate) discussion of the technology. This is a book about the application of IT to the not-for-profit sector.
- If you will run and hide at the first use of any technical term. It is easy to discount almost all writing on IT as 'impenetrable' or 'jargon ridden' if the reader is unwilling to entertain new words and concepts. IT is by nature in part a technical subject. We have tried wherever possible to avoid unnecessary technical terms and to explain less common technical terms within the text.
- If you are going to be disappointed if there are no examples that directly relate to you. Sadly, the market is somewhat limited for a book entitled *IT for animal charities with ten to fifteen staff, a licence for Raisers' Edge and an old version of Sage*. However, if you are in such an organisation, this book should be useful to you if you read it open-mindedly.

Navigating this book

We have set out the book in six parts, five of which reflect the 'Seven Ss' model of organisations and how these relate to IT:

- *IT strategy* – formulating strategies, IT governance, valuing information and knowledge management.
- *IT structure* – history of IT, kit, maintenance and support, security, data protection and health and safety.
- *IT systems* – office tool kits, standard packages, bespoke systems, how to choose and how to implement systems.
- *IT staff and skills* – commitment, use of consultants, training, outsourcing, technophobia and technoscepticism.
- *IT style and shared values* – the internet and world wide web, netiquette, everything that insists on a prefix 'e' and parting thoughts on enjoying your use of IT.

We give some guidance on how to use each part depending on the size of your organisation. The distinction between small, medium-sized and large not-for profit organisations is imprecise and unscientific. The indicators in the table opposite should help, but do bear in mind that complexity can easily be as great a factor as 'numbers of transactions'.

PREFACE TABLE Does size matter?			
Size indicators	Large charity	Medium-sized charity	Small charity
Annual income	£5m or more	£500,000 to £5m	Less than £500,000
Number of staff	200 or more	20 to 200	Fewer than 20
Transactions per year	10,000 or more	500 to 10,000	Fewer than 500
Modules	Ledgers, budgets, job costing, allocations ...	Ledgers and budgets	What's a ledger?
Number of contacts	5,000 or more	300 to 5,000	Fewer than 300
Complexity	Large number of detailed records required on covenants, legacies, membership, sponsorships, donor history, etc	Some detail required in some of the areas listed for larger charities	Detailed aspects tend to be low volume and are reasonably easy to record and manage without complex systems

Each chapter starts with the chapter objectives and ends with a summary of the main points arising. Where relevant, we use figures, tables, templates and checklists and include case examples to illustrate points.

Part six provides some detailed case studies, set out in the five part format described above, with a concluding paragraph on lessons learned.

Appendix A is a 'crystal ball gazing' chapter on where we think the technology is going and the impact those changes might have on the use of IT in the not-for-profit sector within the foreseeable future. Appendix B is a directory suggesting further reading, along some useful addresses and sources of further information.

Over to you

We hope you like the book. We hope it informs you. We hope it helps you to make your organisation more effective. We hope it entertains you.

This is the first edition of this book. We genuinely want to hear and use reader feedback. Your comments will be most welcome and enormously helpful to us for the continuous improvement of future editions of the book. In particular, we are keen to include more case studies in the next edition, especially interesting stories (good and bad) from smaller and medium-sized not-for-profits. Please do contact us with your comments, suggestions and experiences.

Ian Harris and Michael Mainelli
Spring 2001

Acknowledgements

Many thanks to the clients and contacts who kindly gave up their time to help provide case studies, not least:

- Carol Harrison, Bharat Mehta and Tina Stiff at the City Parochial Foundation.
- David Prescott at BEN.
- Nigel Hinks at the Children's Society.
- Fiona Dawe and Anastasia Williams at Youthnet.
- Mike Ward at the Actors' Workshop.
- Ian Theodoresen and Bob Harvey at Barnardo's.

We would also like to thank the Z/Yen people who have helped us with this book in all sorts of ways. At the risk of omitting some who deserve mention, our particular thanks go to Mary O'Callaghan, Jeremy Smith, Sarah-Jane Critchley, Linda Cook, Rakesh Shah, Mishel Vitlov and Marie Logan.

Thanks also to the many resource providers on the web, many of which proved most valuable when researching this book. Where we have borrowed heavily from credited public domain resources, these are duly credited in the main text and/or appendix directory. However, it is the nature of web resources that many sources are incompletely credited or not credited at all. We therefore extend our thanks to all who contribute their information and wisdom to the public domain through the web.

Thanks also to Clare Grist Taylor at ICSA Publishing for tolerating our insistence that our client work needed to take priority over manuscripts and for her gentle persuasion for good changes and deadlines.

Finally, many thanks to our long-suffering partners and families. Janie, Ian's partner, has especially been a 'weekend widow' during this project with remarkable good humour, while Elisabeth, Michael's wife, has given birth to Xenia and Maxine during the conception and birth of this book. Our profound gratitude goes to both Janie and Elisabeth with our solemn promise 'never again, until the next one'.

Introduction

OVERVIEW

This book is about the application of information technology (IT) in the not-for-profit sector. IT is now a pervasive part of the not-for-profit sector for all size of organisations — large, medium-sized, small and tiny. This point was brought home during the writing of this book by the transformation of a friend, outlined in the case example overleaf.

In this introduction, we aim to set the scene in two ways:
- Outlining a number of themes on how not-for-profit organisations can maximise the benefits from their application of IT.
- Sketching some trends in IT that we think will affect the not-for-profit sector within the foreseeable future.

Benefiting from the use of IT

The five themes outlined below, which recur throughout the book, summarise some of the key advice contained herein.

- *Planned use of IT*. Set priorities, separating needs from wants. Most not-for-profit organisations have limited budgets and all not-for-profit organisations are guardians of money that is intended for beneficiaries (not IT per se).
- *Objectives and scope*. Agree objectives and scope of any proposed IT related project. Poorly defined objectives and creeping scope are among the most common reasons for IT implementation failures (real and perceived). Stated more positively, be clear about what you seek from the project, be clear what the project is and then strive hard to achieve your goals.
- *Choosing solutions*. Even if you are a small not-for-profit organisation, you should follow the key steps set out in this book. Scale the level of detail and effort you apply but do not disregard the essence of sensible processes for making good decisions.

CASE EXAMPLE The pervasiveness of IT today

Mike Ward runs a small charitable organisation primarily for the benefit of young people, the Actors' Workshop in Halifax. He is the only employee, there is a board of trustees, a dedicated group of volunteers and a small army of eager young people. Mike, until recently, was one of the least technically minded people we know. Naturally there is some sound and lighting gadgetry at the workshop, but Mike distances himself from that side of things completely – the youngsters know about it and deal with it admirably. In fact, the most 'high tech' device we had seen in his office was the telephone answering machine, followed closely by the electric pencil sharpener.

One day Mike asked about the world wide web because his youngsters were insisting that the workshop should have a web site and e-mail. Further, a local web design company was prepared to help out with a gift-in-kind. What did we think? We told Mike what we thought. He went off looking perplexed. A few weeks later he dropped us a note suggesting that we look at the web site and would we kindly comment on it. We did. A few weeks after that, Mike proudly announced that some kind soul had donated a computer and that he was now on e-mail.

A few months later Mike dropped us another note. The workshop had been burgled just before a show was due to open. The workshop had struggled against all odds (successfully) to beg and borrow enough equipment and facilities ahead of its insurance claim to put on the production. The show had gone on, to fine reviews. But Mike's computer had also been stolen. 'It's terrible', he said, 'I can't get my e-mails until we get a replacement. People keep phoning me and asking why I haven't replied to their e-mails. My only consolation is that the thieves didn't take my electric pencil sharpener.'

Within the space of a few months, Mike had transformed from self-confessed Luddite into a not-for-profit person whose working life depended heavily on the use of IT.

- *Communication, contribution, consensus, commitment.* Ensure that people who are concerned with (or going to be significantly affected by) an IT related project are consulted and involved at appropriate stages. You might be using outside help for the project, but ultimately it is your organisation that has to live with the solution. Ensure that you have planned for sufficient training and skills transfer in the project and keep people informed.
- *Risk/reward management.* Risk/reward management treats all organisational problem solving and decision making as attempts to minimise risks and maximise rewards for the organisation. This risk/reward philosophy pervades the book. We constantly urge the reader to minimise risks (e.g. avoiding bespoke IT solutions if at all possible) and to maximise rewards (e.g. define tangible benefits sought from the IT project and measure results as best you can to ensure that those benefits are achieved).

Twenty-first century trends in IT

While this book is not really about the technology per se, it is helpful to understand those trends that are likely to be important to not-for-profit organisations. Chapters such as 'E-verything' and appendix A cover these aspects in a little more depth. We have grouped our thoughts into five main trends:

- *Smaller, faster, cheaper.* Technology has consistently doubled in power and halved in price every eighteen months since the mid 1960s. Even the old, donated computer referred to in this introduction's case example has as much or more computing processing power than all the computer processing power used to put the Apollo 11 astronauts on the moon in 1969. This trend in improved power is likely to continue for the foreseeable future, and it increases possibilities for the not-for-profit sector. As a technology becomes commoditised, and therefore affordable to most people, even the tiniest not-for-profit organisation can consider whether that technology could help them.
- *Ever widening world.* As computers and networks become ubiquitous, the application of IT for not-for-profit organisations moves away from the office and into the field. For example, expect to see more and more demand for field workers, activists and volunteers to use hand-held devices and/or short text messaging devices to communicate with your offices and with each other.
- *IT as a utility.* Commercial offerings are starting to focus on service provision and reliability. The web enables suppliers to deliver services to organisations in new ways. For example, application service providers can offer IT applications on a pay-as-you-go basis. This can help not-for-profit organisations with limited capital budgets and/or uncertainty with regard to expected growth.
- *Relationship management.* Commercial organisations are increasingly using IT to manage their relationships with their customers. Again, the development of models for trading over the world wide web have hastened the development of such recording, profiling and tracking systems. Not-for-profit organisations should expect to see parallel developments, for example in beneficiary relationship management and donor relationship management.
- *Human–machine interface advances.* Speech recognition has been steadily improving in quality and reducing in price – anticipate seeing this technology really take off in the next few years in the not-for-profit sector, for both management and service

provision work. New interface areas are still more in the laboratory than the not-for-profit organisation, but the curious should look out for holograms, smell interfaces, direct brain connections, wearable computers, whole-body sensors and the like. Expect also to see increasing emphasis on 3D visualisation and predictive modelling. While this paragraph might seem mostly 'in the future', we expect to see several of these technologies having real, practical case studies illustrating uses in the not-for-profit sector in future editions of this book. So keep an eye on the trends.

Part 1

IT strategy

IT strategy – Using this part of the book

This is probably the most narrative part of the book although it also contains plenty of practical tips and techniques for producing an IT strategy for your organisation. For example, 'Needs, wants and prioritisation' contains tools for determining information needs and prioritising your ideas and the COD-VERB table in 'Governance' provides a useful checklist to ensure that you are getting value from your use of IT.

If you are interested in larger not-for-profit organisations or a student of management, you will probably find the whole part useful and pertinent.

If you are interested in smaller and medium-sized not-for-profit organisations, you will probably benefit from reading 'IT strategy: what and why' for context and using 'Needs, wants and prioritisation' and the first part of 'Governance' as practical guides to formulating your IT strategy. You will also get some thoughts and ideas from skimming the second part of 'Governance' and 'Knowledge management'.

IT strategy: what and why

CHAPTER OBJECTIVES

In this chapter we shall:

- Define strategy and IT strategy.
- Discuss the relationship between organisational strategy and IT strategy.
- Explain why IT strategy is important to all organisations.

What is strategy?

The word 'strategy' comes from a Greek word, *strategos*, which means a military general. Early strategies were generals' plans and it can be a little unnerving in the not-for-profit sector to indulge in an activity which so obviously originated for military purposes. However, organisational strategy has moved on from the military style. It has also, thankfully, mostly moved on from the rah-rah approach of hollow vision and mission statements designed to rally the workforce.

A strategy can be defined as an 'integrated set of actions to achieve sustainable competitive advantage'. Whereas in the past strategy has often been seen as synonymous with long-range planning as opposed to short-term planning, today we tend to look at strategy as the means of making high-risk, high-reward decisions rather than day-to-day decisions.

The diagram overleaf illustrates four types of decision, only one of which is strategic:

- *Low risk, low reward* decisions are tactical.
- *High risk, low reward* decisions are about strategic assumptions (e.g. risk management).

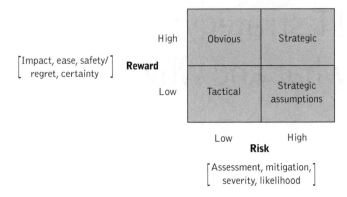

FIGURE 1.1 Risk/reward strategy diagam

- *Low risk, high reward* decisions are obvious.
- *High risk, high reward* decisions are strategic.

How does one strategise?

Strategy could be the subject of a book in its own right. We present below an illustration of a typical risk/reward approach to strategy, using the Z/Ealous risk/reward methodology for a quasi-government, not-for-profit client. For a large organisation, such an exercise can involve many weeks of work. Smaller organisations can achieve excellent results following the same approach in a handful of thoughtful sessions.

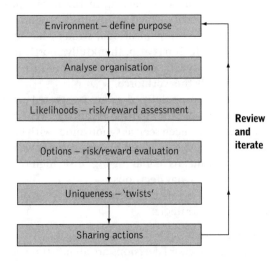

FIGURE 1.2 Z/Ealous risk/reward strategy

The phases

- *Environment*: the team confirmed its objectives, the organisation's mission, goals, values and beliefs e.g. public sector values, private sector involvement. It also developed some generic risk/reward 'trees' (cascading sets of risk/reward structures) from research on similar organisations.
- *Analysis*: a variety of strategic planning tools, e.g. Porter's five forces, BCG models and factor analysis, were used to find the risk/reward issues that affected the organisation in achieving its mission. All issues were valid, even though later ranking of severity and likelihoods might diminish the importance of some. A unique risk/reward tree was built for the organisation (see figure 1.3), with political risk as the root risk and meeting charitable objectives as the root reward.
- *Likelihoods (risk/reward)*: forty to fifty major issues were categorised as risks or rewards. Risk/reward issues were also reversed (risks became rewards and vice versa) to determine the full shape of the possible outcomes, as perceived by senior managers. Taking the final set of issues and their possible outcomes, a Monte Carlo simulation was run, combining the risks and rewards with their severities and likelihoods, identifying those which had the greatest impact on the organisation either achieving or failing in its goals.
- *Options*: for each issue, a variety of actions was developed, and a variety of actions, that senior managers hoped to achieve, e.g. Investors in People, were correlated, if possible, with risk/reward issues. Options were ranked on categories such as impact, certainty, safety/regret and ease.
- *Uniqueness*: both the risk/reward issues and the options for addressing them were then subjected to finding the 'twist', i.e. a way of succinctly expressing the issues and options that revealed their underlying essence. The 'issues twist' was a short tale describing the scenario of the organisation. The 'options twist' was an easily remembered five-point strategy subsuming almost a hundred separate actions.
- *Sharing*: the issues were shared with the organisation and its stakeholders. The actions were partially re-discovered and partially re-worked with the stakeholders, including more junior management. The strategy was implemented as both a hard system, i.e. corporate plan and objectives, and a soft system, i.e. culture change to achieve greater unity in both risk/reward beliefs and their priorities. Results, both successes and failures, were tracked and fed into the subsequent year's planning cycle.

A possible risk/reward tree for a not-for-profit organisation is illustrated below.

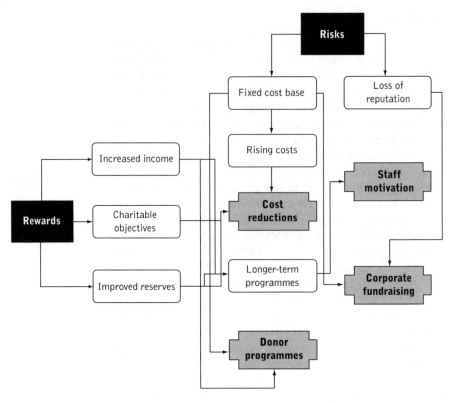

FIGURE 1.3 Risk/reward trees

The important point is that any strategy, be it an organisational one, a reserves strategy or an IT strategy, can follow the above basic process to good effect and that phases can be repeated as needed.

Further, there is a relationship between IT strategy and organisational strategy. How IT strategy relates to an organisation's strategy can be a matter of debate and is discussed further below.

What is an IT strategy?

IT strategy can be defined as 'the alignment of an organisation's goals with the planned use of IT within the organisation'. The processes of an IT strategy can be summarised as:

- Understanding the organisation and its objectives.
- Identifying information needs (separating needs from wants).
- Prioritising IT opportunities within the constraints of your available resources.

The challenges for not-for-profit organisations in tackling these processes successfully are discussed in the next chapter.

It might seem arcane to discuss the relationship between organisational and IT strategy at some length, but it is in fact important. If you have not worked out how you are planning to align your organisation's use of IT with its goals, you don't really know where to begin planning your use of IT. We believe that there are essentially four main ways in which an organisation can relate its business (organisational) strategy to its IT strategy:

1 *Independent.* Organisational strategy and IT strategy are developed independently of one another and subsequently aligned.
2 *Hierarchical.* The IT strategy is one of several 'departmental' strategies subservient to the organisational strategy. Such an IT strategy would be established after (and as a result of) an organisational strategy.
3 *Subset.* The IT strategy is an intrinsic subset of the organisational strategy. Such an IT strategy would probably be formulated along with the organisational strategy.
4 *Multi-functions.* Several IT strategies co-exist – each of the organisation's business functions has its own IT strategy. Such a collection of strategies would probably be developed individually and quite possibly in an uncoordinated manner.

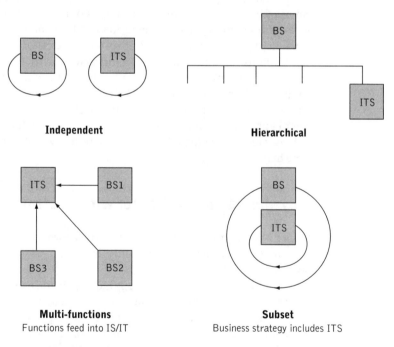

FIGURE 1.4 IT strategy integration

Several years ago we conducted a survey of several hundred organisations, mostly commercial, some governmental, some voluntary sector. We asked (amongst other things) about the nature of

TABLE 1.1 IT strategy types survey results

IT strategy type	All sector survey early 90s: percentage of respondees	Recent voluntary sector survey: percentage of respondees
Independent	6	5
Hierarchical	42	25
Subset	40	65
Multi-functions	12	5

the relationship between their IT strategy and organisational strategy. In our recent survey of the voluntary sector we asked this question again. The results are shown in table 1.1, above.

We do not believe that there are right and wrong answers to this question, as different organisations have different structures and needs. We find it unlikely that many organisations would benefit from undertaking IT strategy in isolation from organisational strategy (type 1), but the other three types of relationship can be effective in the right circumstances. Where not-for-profit organisations often err is by being too quick to adopt a multi-function (type 4) approach to IT strategy on the basis (for example) that fundraising is a fundamentally different activity from service provision or grant making. Most not-for-profit organisations would benefit more from a single IT strategy that brings together common IT needs and themes. This approach helps an organisation to improve information sharing across its diverse functions, making hierarchical (type 2) or subset (type 3) style IT strategies more helpful candidates.

Why should anyone bother with IT strategy?

At one level, IT strategy is easy. We can write a form of IT strategy for your organisation without even meeting you. So why bother to devise your own?

At a more realistic level, IT strategy is difficult and can be especially hard for not-for-profit organisations. We tend to describe IT strategy as 'the slightly scientific art of exploring IT aspirations and containing them within pragmatic, prioritised plans for using IT to support your not-for-profit organisation's business strategy'. The output should be an integrated and achievable set of actions. Not-for-profit organisations often have high aspirations and very limited means to fulfil those aspirations. Common resource constraints in not-for-profits (not enough money, not

CASE EXAMPLE   The never-ending, ideal IT strategy

'Our organisation would like instant access at the touch of just one button (or the bark of a single command) from any location to all of the organisation's own information and any conceivable external information source. All possible elements of the system should be fully integrated.

The systems should be available to all but it should be possible to secure information by restricting access at an infinite number of levels. The systems should be 100 per cent stable and completely reliable. All at negligible cost.'

enough people, cannot be seen to be spending too much on technology) are all the more reason to do some IT strategic thinking.

Most not-for-profit organisations are using IT to some extent. Almost all of those organisations could better support their business strategy simply by applying their existing IT more appropriately to their needs. Often, a small investment in some additional IT can 'get most of the way' to meeting needs, whereas the 'whiz bang' solution that would meet all the needs is beyond the organisation's means. All too often, opportunities to 'get most of the way' towards the not-for-profit organisation's aims are wasted due to the futile search for an affordable 'whiz bang' solution. A good IT strategy will retain the vision or aspirations, explore the opportunities available and come up with practical, achievable plans for action which support the organisation's strategic objectives.

We believe that an organisation should revise its IT strategy whenever it revises its business strategy. IT strategies tend to date within two to three years, so if strategic planning is irregular in your organisation, consider reviewing your IT strategy in between business strategies. For large not-for-profit organisations (possibly forty to fifty of the largest UK charities and trusts), the effort involved in IT strategy might be several weeks' work. For most not-for-profit organisations, the effort involved is anything from one day to a few days' work. The benefits can often flow quickly and reward the effort many times over.

Summary

- A strategy is an integrated set of actions to achieve an organisation's goals.
- Large and small organisations can use a similar approach to producing a strategy – the same basic approach can be used for organisational and IT strategy.

- IT strategy is the alignment of the organisation's use of it with those goals.
- In most not-for-profit organisations, IT strategy should be devised in conjunction with the organisation's strategy or in the aftermath of an organisation's strategic review.
- One of the biggest challenges for not-for-profit organisations is separating IT needs from IT wants in order to prioritise the use of limited resources to achieve strategic goals (see the next chapter).
- All not-for-profit organisations should benefit from undertaking IT strategy on a sensible scale at fairly regular intervals (every two to four years).

Needs, wants and prioritisation

CHAPTER OBJECTIVES

In this chapter we shall:

- Worry about the fact that so many IT strategies are unachievable.
- Illustrate tools and techniques for separating needs from wants.
- Provide you with tips on prioritising IT opportunities within the constraints of your achievable resources.

What can really be done?

So many IT strategies that we see are unachievable wish lists. We frequently come across IT strategies that read a little like the spoof strategy in chapter 1, often in small not-for-profit organisations with limited resources that couldn't possibly achieve the ivory tower ideas.

The following case example is one of several in the book, which are reminiscent of actual examples the authors have come across.

Tools and techniques

There are many tools and techniques available to help with IT strategies. In part 4 we discuss communication, contribution, consensus and commitment (the 'four Cs') in more detail. Suffice to say here that experience teaches us that the more collaborative and consultative techniques tend to be especially effective in the not-for-profit sector as long as the tools are applied well. Table 2.1 (page 17) contains a non-exhaustive list, but includes the main tools we have found effective.

CASE EXAMPLE Save our Sprats

A well-meaning trustee of 'Save our Sprats' (SOS), a small but excellent charity, knew someone who was very high up in 'MegaITcorp inc' (Mega). Mega is well known for building mission critical trading systems for the world's biggest banks and exchanges. Generously, Mega assigned one of its top business analysts to SOS to help it with its IT strategy. The analyst was a bright young thing, but she had never looked at any organisation employing fewer than 1000 people and used the term 'small budget' to mean anything between £100,000 and £500,000. Both of SOS's finance people were open-minded and keen to benefit from Mega's generous support. SOS employed twenty-five people and when the finance people used the term 'small budget' they meant under £1000.

The finance people were frank with the analyst, so she quickly identified that SOS found it problematic to match calls for funding with its available restricted and unrestricted funds. (Commodities traders have analogous problems matching tradable warrants with commodity trades.) There were relatively cheap packages available which could help with this problem. When the analyst said 'this package is cheap' she meant that a starter pack software licence could be had for £50,000 to £100,000. When the head of finance heard 'the package is cheap' he hoped the analyst meant less

than £100, although he had a sneaking suspicion that this 'city type' analyst might mean as much as £500. 'We'll probably need a day or two's training as well, so better put aside £1500', he thought.

Each limb of the IT strategy was developed in the same way, until it all came tumbling down when SOS woke up to the price ticket on some of the more alluring ideas. Strangely, because the analyst had no experience of work with similar organisations, those more alluring ideas were probably wants more than needs – more immediate possible 'quick wins' were overlooked in the flurry. Equally strangely, the Mega analyst's experience in large financial organisations could have been incredibly useful to SOS if her knowledge had been tempered with an understanding of SOS's context. Going back to the matching funds example, a day's work sitting alongside the accountant prototyping a spreadsheet model for matching funds would have delivered most of the benefits within the constraints of SOS's budget.

Result: 'the information we have isn't the information we want, the information we want isn't the information we need, the information we need isn't available'. When you hear this mantra (or its equivalent), you know it's time to revise your IT strategy to take appropriate account of needs, wants and priorities.

Critical sets

As an example, figure 2.1 (page 18) shows the critical sets model. A charity needs sets of information to help it to measure whether it is meeting critical success factors (e.g. fundraising targets, number of people cared for). It also needs sets of information to help it validate critical assumptions (e.g. the extent to which a disease is

TABLE 2.1 Tools and techniques

Tool / technique	Main purpose / description	Collaborative/ consultative?	Other comments
Interviews (technique)	■ Understanding objectives ■ Identifying information needs ■ Prioritising IT opportunities	Consultative	Time consuming
Focus groups (technique)	■ Understanding objectives ■ Identifying information needs ■ Prioritising IT opportunities	Collaborative and consultative	Popular and effective for charities
Six thinking hats	■ Encourage people to think broadly ■ Initiate brainstorming	Collaborative	Good ice breaker (e.g. where focus groups are rarely used)
Five forces models	■ Helps to understand uniqueness and comparative advantage ■ Stems from 'competitor' analysis	Collaborative	Can be applied to many voluntary sector situations, but should be used selectively
Value chains	■ Understanding objectives	Collaborative and/or consultative	Values can be comparatively complex for charities
Critical sets	■ Identifying information needs	Collaborative and/or consultative	Often effective in focus groups – a key tool for IT strategy
High-level data models	■ Identifying information needs	Consultative	Usually used to confirm rather than devise
Potential IT opportunities	■ Input for prioritising IT opportunities	Consultative	Often used to confirm and expand list rather than to initiate
Ranking	■ Prioritising IT opportunities	Collaborative and/or consultative	Often effective for reaching consensus on priorities, helping to gain commitment

becoming more or less prevalent in society, poverty demographics) and to help evaluate critical decisions (e.g. how many more nurses will we need in our care home this year, should we do a mail shot or put on a special event with our remaining budget?). You can use the templates below figure 2.1 to identify your main information needs in each of the sets (i.e. factors, assumptions, decisions). Focus groups can be a valuable way of identifying the key information needs in each of these sets and in helping people within the organisation to understand its differing information needs and varying purposes for information use. This form of analysis also helps organisations to divide up their information needs into definable and manageable chunks, e.g. horizon scanning systems to help assess critical decisions and management information systems to help measure critical success factors.

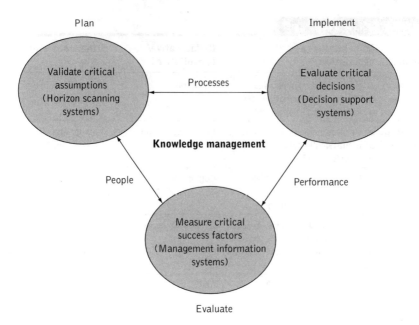

FIGURE 2.1 Critical information sets

TEMPLATE 2.1 Critical success factors

Critical success factor	Aspect of business	Why critical?

TEMPLATE 2.2 Critical assumptions

Critical assumption	Information needed	Source/value

TEMPLATE 2.3 Critical decisions

Critical decision	Information needed	Timeliness

Ranking and prioritising IT opportunities

Once your IT strategy exercise has generated a long list of things you want, you need to prioritise the ideas and decide which actions you are actually going to take. A simple tool to help with prioritisation is ranking. You force participants to rank the items on the wish list. An example is set out in table 2.2, below.

This form of ranking, simple though it is:

- Helps to stimulate discussion and debate.
- Ensures that participants pay at least some attention to all items.
- Helps the development of consensus.
- Shows participants that other parts of the organisation have different priorities.
- Focuses attention on the high priority opportunities.

There are risks to using ranking, not least:

- A false sense of scientific validity, as samples are often small, the judgement applied subjective and the options are not always clearly defined.
- Not all opinions have equal weight, but it would be courageous of you to try and weight the responses by seniority or depth of understanding!
- The answers are rarely conclusive. Having said that, the use of the second ranking column in the table above, 'priority for the organisation as a whole', sometimes uncovers a remarkable level of consensus in not-for-profit organisations, where people have a propensity to think in terms of the common good.

One further step is to get people to think realistically about possible speed of action. It might be possible to tackle a relatively low

TABLE 2.2 Ranking table

IT opportunity	Priority for me personally	Priority for the organisation as a whole
Replacing the finance system before it falls over	4	3
An intranet for staff directory and collaborative working	3	4
Enhancing the fundraising system so we can get reports out	2	2
Providing record management software for care provision services	6	1
WAP phones for all field fundraisers and fundraising managers	1	5
Replacing the grants administration system before it falls over	5	6
... etc.		

Rank the IT opportunities set out in the table, 1 = the most important, 6 = the least important

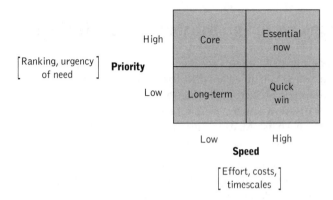

FIGURE 2.2 Priority and speed diagram

priority item and get a 'quick win', because that particular opportunity is low cost and low effort. In the example above, the basic intranet opportunity might be relatively quick and easy to achieve (assuming the infrastructure is in place), whereas the replacement of the finance system is likely to take a good deal longer. These projects could perhaps take place in parallel. Figure 2.2, above, illustrates some of the thinking you might do with regard to priority and speed.

To record your deliberations, you might set out your analysis under the following headings:

- *Possible action*: state the action you are considering.
- *Further thoughts*: implementation considerations.
- *Onus*: who is going to own this action.
- *Priority*: how high a priority is this action.
- *Speed*: how quickly do you need this action implemented.
- *Estimated costs (ranges)*: how much it will cost you.
- *Estimated benefits (ranges)*: what are the tangible benefits of the action.
- *Estimated effort (ranges):* how many days' work is involved.

Such a template might form the basis of your financial planning and is well on the way to being an outline action plan once your work programme is agreed. In larger organisations, your deliberations over the budgeting and project planning will of course go into more detail. For smaller organisations, analysis at this level can be a very useful route map for many months or even years.

Summary

- Make sure your IT strategy is realistic and achievable.
- Encourage participants to be clear about what they need and what they want.

- There are many tools and techniques available to help you – we've listed many you can try.
- Critical sets is an especially useful tool to get people thinking clearly about their information needs.
- Ranking can help to build consensus and manage the thorny issues around prioritisation.
- When formulating your plans, remember that some opportunities are easier to achieve than others – such factors should inform your planning.
- This is not 'ivory tower' strategy – the results of such an exercise should be a pragmatic action plan for a hugely beneficial programme of work.

Governance

CHAPTER OBJECTIVES

In this chapter we shall:

- Explain the distinction between information systems and IT infrastructure, why it is important and how to define both.
- Discuss issues relating to paying for IT, including authorisation, cost allocations and capital versus expenditure.
- Raise the matter of co-ordinating the use of IT, including setting and controlling IT standards.
- Provide some examples of how not-for-profit organisations deal with the governance of their information systems and IT infrastructure.
- Encourage not-for-profit organisations to try to value the benefits of IT.
- Explain why there is no such thing as a free lunch when using IT.
- Borrow valuation techniques from the world of audit and basic finance in order to help value those benefits.
- Categorise the risks and rewards of information and knowledge management.

Information systems and IT infrastructure

There is an important distinction between information systems and IT infrastructure. Information systems are the applications through which we record, process and present data in the form of information. IT infrastructure is the collection of mechanisms that receive, store and transmit data to enable the information systems. In summary; information systems are the user programs, IT infrastructure is the machines, networks and enabling software. A domestic analogy: information systems are the equivalent of domestic electrical appliances whereas IT infrastructure is the equivalent of the electrical cabling.

There are several reasons why the distinction between information systems and IT infrastructure is important:

- The skills required to manage information systems are different from the skills needed to manage IT infrastructure.
- It usually makes sense for different parts of an organisation to manage or 'own' the systems and the infrastructure. For example, specific departments often 'own' the systems (e.g. the fundraising department 'owns' the fundraising system and finance 'owns' the accounting system, whereas the support services department 'owns' the IT infrastructure).
- Processes within systems and the data within systems should all have clear ownership. For example, systems that cover more than one department (often a recipe for unclear ownership) should at least have clear ownership of processes and data identifiable down to departments, projects, units or whatever.
- Governance mechanisms for investment and ongoing expenditure on information technology is likely to differ between spend on information systems (which is usually attributable to one or two functions or departments) and spend on IT infrastructure (which is essentially a shared resource across the whole organisation).
- The distinction has an impact on who pays (or should pay) for the particular bit of IT (see 'Who pays?', below) and who takes responsibility for co-ordination (see 'Co-ordination aspects of governance', below).

Distinguishing between information systems and IT infrastructure

Table 3.1, overleaf, should help you to distinguish between information systems and IT structure, as well as highlight the main 'grey areas'. The trick is to ensure that your organisation has clear definitions and allocates management, ownership and governance sensibly and unambiguously.

Who pays?

Once you have sorted out these relationships the answer to the question 'who pays?' should be simple – the owner. If you are spending money on a particular application, the user department(s) involved should pick up the tab.

TABLE 3.1 Information systems and IT infrastructure

Function	IT infrastructure	Information systems
Wide area network (WAN)	✓	
Central processors	✓	
Local area networks (LANs)	✓	
Departmental file servers	✓	
Network systems administration	✓	
Local network printers	✓	
Electronic 'desktop' (e.g. PC on desk)	✓	
Network operating systems	✓	
Electronic 'desktop' operating systems	✓	
E-mail system	✓	
Desktop tools (e.g. wordprocessor, spreadsheet, presentation tools)	✓	? some small systems
Desktop database tool(s)		✓
Corporate macros and templates	✓?	✓?
Corporate database tool(s)	✓	
Corporate data structures	✓?	✓?
Corporate data systems administration	✓	
Departmental applications		✓
Corporate data	✓?	✓?
Departmental data		✓
IT help desk	✓	
IT training	✓?	✓?
Interfaces between corporate and departmental applications	✓?	✓?

Many not-for-profit organisations need to consider the extent to which funding partners should be expected to share the cost of IT. This is especially important for service-providing organisations, where IT costs can form a substantial proportion of the costs of projects. It is a fairly common mistake to minimise or avoid cost allocation, only to find that IT costs (perhaps erroneously deemed to be central) are escalating rapidly with no corresponding source of funding to maintain services.

The authorisation for spending on IT should normally follow the same rules as you have for other items in your organisation. IT expenditure is prone to 'fudging' between capital and revenue definitions, so your rules should be simple and clear.

There are no right answers and few wrong answers to the question of what you should treat as capital and what you should treat

> **CASE EXAMPLE**   Capital or expenditure?
>
> At Z/Yen we treat new IT equipment (e.g. portable computers, servers, routers) as capital to be written off over three years. Operating systems software (e.g. Windows 2000) is deemed to be part of the equipment for the purposes of capitalising, budgeting, authorisation and accounting policy. Applications software (e.g. Office 2000, Quickbooks, Crystal Ball) and accessories (e.g. portable computer carry cases, modems, removable drives) are treated as expenditure and written off in the year the expenditure is incurred. However, we could just as easily capitalise applications software or treat operating systems software as expenditure. Similarly, we deem anti virus software and e-mail software upgrades to be applications and therefore expenditure, but we could deem them to be operating systems and therefore capital spend.

as expenditure. For example, many organisations choose to capitalise the cost of their IT application systems.

If you are recharging IT costs to user departments, you should consider whether this recharge is simply an allocation of budgets and costs or a genuine attempt to provide user departments with choices. For example, should the department spend the money on IT rather than on other things? Should the organisation procure IT centrally or allow decentralised procurement? This leads to the issue of co-ordination.

Co-ordination aspects of governance

There is a paradox in the concept of user choice. In principle, you want users to have maximum freedom of choice in systems and structure. In practice, if you allow everyone to do their own thing you'll get a proliferation of incompatible systems and equipment which can quickly become uncontrollable and unaffordable – and so end up restricting users' choice.

Whoever is responsible for the IT infrastructure should also have a clear responsibility to co-ordinate IT standards within the organisation. This is not a 'just say no' responsibility, but a genuine and sometimes difficult role to try and resolve the paradox of choice versus standards. Similarly, in organisations that use standard application systems in multiple locations, whoever is responsible for the application system should co-ordinate those software standards.

Standard and non-standard software

Here are some guidelines on the use of standard and non-standard software:

- Where both the standard application and an alternative solution are able to meet the need, you should choose the solution that is simplest to manage (which would normally be the standard application).
- An alternative solution to the standard application should only be accepted if there is a significant requirement which it cannot meet. It should be up to the proposer of the alternative solution to demonstrate that the standard application is inadequate, as the cost and resource implications where alternative solutions are used are considerable. For example, it should not be sufficient that an alternative solution is a little easier or more convenient for one or two individuals; the 'common good' within the organisation should take precedence.
- If an alternative solution is chosen, data from that solution should be available in the standard format to enable the consolidation, aggregation and comparison of information across the organisation.
- In order to evaluate the use of an alternative solution, the full cost to both the user department/project/unit and to the organisation as a whole over the life of the implementation should be evaluated. The department/project/unit should demonstrate that the benefits of the proposed alternative solution outweigh those total costs.
- Where a project is a joint venture, the situation may arise where more than one organisation wishes the information systems to follow its standards. In such a case, the organisation should negotiate for the use of its standard application. Should an alternative system be chosen for joint work, the organisation should seek appropriate financial compensation to enable it to meet its own information needs as well as those of the venture and to cover any additional costs and effort involved as a result of such a decision.
- A truly single user application, e.g. special software for one person working alone, can be viewed as a pilot.
- In other circumstances, the use of non-standard software should be prohibited, in line with the organisation's general policies on the use of non-standard software and hardware.

Examples of structuring for IT governance

Co-ordinating structures should reflect the ownership and relationships between information systems and IT infrastructure. In larger not-for-profit organisations this is likely to involve several groups. For smaller and medium-sized organisations, this will probably involve a fairly simple and occasional (usually at budgeting time) liaison group to ensure that those responsible for IT

CASE EXAMPLE Barnardo's IT governance structure

At Barnardo's, IT governance is vested essentially with three groups:

- A forward looking IT strategy group (including some representatives from industry) to ensure that there is appropriate long-term planning for IT infrastructure to meet likely demand for information systems.
- A group of senior people from user departments primarily responsible for prioritising information systems requests and co-ordinating (i.e. ensuring that there is appropriate liaison between) new information systems projects.
- A user group to ensure that the user voice is heard. In large organisations (Barnardo's employs several thousand people) it is impractical to consult everyone on IT matters, so a representative body is appropriate.

Ian Theodoreson, Director of Finance and Corporate Services, comments 'even within the clear division of roles between information systems and IT infrastructure there is a dilemma. How can the project leader in any one of Barnardo's 250 project sites around the country really feel as if they "own" the applications? Someone has to make the decision to go ahead and spend often considerable sums of money, and this decision cannot be taken on the basis of consensus opinion. The balancing factor therefore has to be the establishment of a clearly focused user group, drawing membership from across the organisation, who can identify the issues and needs that are arising and who can moderate initiatives that are emanating from the centre'.

infrastructure have the budget and capability to provide the IT infrastructure needed for proposed information systems changes.

At a medium-sized not-for-profit organisation such as BEN (see part 6), IT governance is essentially vested with the directors. In addition, a group of staff from user departments meet a few times a year to co-ordinate IT activity and ensure that an appropriate level of service is maintained.

In small organisations, IT governance is likely to be covered by the executive(s) on a more ad hoc basis, but the above principles should nevertheless apply.

The cost of everything and the value of nothing

Governance of IT can be seen as four main areas:

- Agreeing who owns IT.
- Agreeing who pays for IT.
- Co-ordinating IT.
- Valuing IT.

We have discussed ownership, payment and co-ordination, but not yet valuing IT. There are many derogatory expressions about people who know the cost of everything and the value of nothing. Sadly, IT is an area where this expression is often true; many not-for-profit organisations put a great deal of effort into estimating the cost of IT projects and trying to manage those costs, but few try to value the benefits they are seeking from IT. If your organisation falls into this category, you are probably missing a trick or two.

Understanding the value of IT

Often not-for-profit organisations pay lip service to phrases such as 'information is an asset' and 'the benefits of information'. To move away from lip service, in other words really to try to understand value of IT, think of the audit as an analogy for valuing IT. For any significant asset, an auditor expects seven typical pieces of evidence:

- Accurate understanding of the **C**ost of the asset.
- Confirmation of **O**wnership of the asset.
- Some **D**isclosure of the importance of the asset.
- Ability to confirm the **V**alue of the asset.
- Evidence of the **E**xistence of the asset.
- Clear lines of **R**esponsibility for the asset.
- Measurable **B**enefit from the asset.

The surreal, but snappy, phrase 'COD-VERB' is already catching on as a mnemonic device. Without all of the above, phrases such as 'information as an asset' or 'knowledge management' are just fluff sitting on top of some new technology. Meeting the above tests should be a goal for most not-for-profit organisations when considering applying funds to IT projects. Examining each of the seven factors in turn, we can see how leading organisations are starting to put weight behind the concept of knowledge value. Table 3.2 proposes some tests for each factor.

There's no such thing as a free lunch

You hardly need to be told that not-for-profit organisations often lack some of the resources (skills and/or money) required to plan, implement and evaluate a desired or needed IT solution. They often find themselves in the (seemingly fortunate) position of being offered some voluntary help with the IT project, which may be in the form of goods (equipment), services (advice, skills) or both. Such help may seem like manna from heaven but it might

TABLE 3.2 COD-VERB

Factor	Questions	Evidence
Cost	■ How much has it cost to build? ■ How much does it cost to maintain? ■ What are the indirect costs of IT, i.e. how much are our people creating in the course of doing work and how much activity is specifically for information enhancement?	■ Specific numbers in the management accounts ■ Activity-based costing analysis of information acquisition, interpretation, storage and renewal ■ Qualitative statements which analyse the information created during assignments
Ownership	■ Do we have clear title to our information and/or systems? ■ Do we know what bought knowledge is crucial? ■ Is our data more or less valuable than externally benchmarked information bases?	■ Copyrights, trademarks, documented methodologies ■ Maps to data and information sources ■ Regular challenges of external data costs; frequent comparisons of information sources and usefulness
Disclosure	■ Do we publish a value? ■ Could we defend a minimum value?	■ Appraisals of the IT projects ■ Annual reviews of information based achievements
Value	■ Do we have a valuation methodology for our information? ■ Do we measure the increase in value? ■ Is the value of information part of our economic value added measures? ■ Do other people value our information?	■ Clear descriptions of how information adds value to people and processes ■ Agonising over the value of information to be published ■ Licensing fees, usage charges, database swaps
Existence	■ Do we audit our data for completeness, accuracy and location? ■ Do we have procedures to control major changes in our data? ■ Can we point to information which is 'retired' (not just archived)?	■ Frequent information 'raids' ■ Use of external information auditors ■ Statistics on average use, lifecycle times, data demographics, ageing statistics ■ Data mortality analysis
Responsibility	■ Can senior management find this knowledge that they talk about? ■ Is someone in charge of the value of all organisational knowledge? ■ Is someone responsible for each major area of information, its quality, maintenance and development?	■ Management usage time ■ People being held accountable for falls in information value ■ Contention over who gets to update IT systems areas
Benefit	■ Are our people (managers) willing to pay from their budgets for access and usage? ■ Can we demonstrate that our charity has competitive advantage?	■ Disputes over internal costings for IT use – any charges for IT access ■ Awards, citations or other qualitative measures vis-à-vis other charities in similar areas of work

be a poisoned chalice. Strangely, commercial organisations are rarely offered voluntary help in this way.

This is not to say that you should never accept gifts of IT equipment and services, indeed some not-for-profits have done remarkable things as a result of gifts in kind (see the Youthnet case study in part 6). However, you should examine the situation very carefully before accepting a gift which might not be appropriate for you. The table below raises some of the issues to consider when considering accepting the types of voluntary help that are commonly offered.

The key thing to consider is the value you will get from the project you are undertaking. Very often, however, not-for-profit organisations undertake projects needlessly in order to take advantage of a 'gift', ignoring the hidden costs, such as effort, upgrades to peripheral equipment etc. Also, organisations often accept gifts without realising that there are hidden costs and risks associated with the gift itself which nullify or even outweigh its value. Gifts of old equipment frequently fall into this category. If a gift directly supports a project which you had intended to pay for anyway and does not generate hidden costs or risks that outweigh its value, then the gift might be a bonus for you. In our experience, such gifts are rare.

TABLE 3.3 No such thing as a free lunch

Type of free lunch sought	Issues	Comments, matters to consider
General	Conflict of interest	Take care if the donor or advisor has a vested interest in the solution (e.g. free consultancy from a software supplier)
	Market value	Understand the market value of the gift and its significance to the overall solution
	Restricted choice	Beware gifts that restrict your choice of other aspects of the solution (e.g. of hardware and software)
	Maintenance	Only accept gifts of hardware and software that can be properly upgraded, supported and maintained
Equipment	Age and history of equipment	Be cautious of equipment that is old (two years can be old) Also be cautious of second hand equipment (why does the original owner no longer want it?)
Software	Match with requirements	Consider using free software only if you would have been prepared to pay for it Do not use software illegally, however impecunious you might be
Advice and implementation assistance	Value	Will you value advice if it is free?
	Skills requirement	Do the skills of the volunteer really match your current requirements?
	Commitment	Is the volunteer committed to getting things done and seeing their part of the project through?

The economics of valuation

Valuation binds all seven factors of asset management. Without value, assets are meaningless. The value of information is a much bandied about concept. As with other intangible assets, such as brands, knowledge values are still somewhat uncertain but, as techniques spread and more comparisons of value become available, confidence and usage will rise rapidly. The demand for better measures of knowledge rises as donors and other stakeholders rightly require managers to justify the commitment of more and more capital to knowledge-intensive projects.

Some basic economics can help. Value is often perhaps best tested by seeing what some people are prepared to pay and what others expect to charge. Economic theory indicates that competitive pricing will drive prices (and therefore perceived value) close to each other if competing 'suppliers' have 'perfect information' about the markets, products and/or services which they supply and demand. It is this theory that leads you to use competitive tendering to choose systems (see chapter 14). You can use the same type of thinking to value the entire initiative. Would it be cheaper and better to buy in the service, the system or the information we want from a third party supplier rather than go to the bother of implementing systems ourselves? The advent of so many application service providers (ASPs), who provide just such third party services, often on a pay-as-you-go basis, indicates that IT suppliers believe that they have spotted an economic trend. With the world wide web as a possible delivery mechanism for applications, many organisations will find it more cost effective and beneficial to source the entire application and/or information provision from a third party supplier than to undertake the initiative themselves in the traditional manner.

However, there are even more discriminating ways of assessing value than relying solely on competition theory and pay-as-you-go data charges for application services. Often, the perceived value (or lack of value) in an IT initiative arises during the initiative rather than in the initial proposition. In other words, the huge cost overrun or the hugely beneficial spin-off arises while the project is running.

Basic economics can also help us to scope, control and value IT projects as they are going along. If we can estimate the marginal benefits and costs of additional information, which might or might not form part of the initiative, we ought to be able to decide whether the additional information will provide net value. This might sound theoretical, but in our experience successful IT projects have to grapple with practical decisions around extending the scope of the initiative almost from day one.

Each rescoping decision should involve some thinking about the net value (marginal benefits and costs) likely to arise from that decision. Whilst we accept that it is not possible to compute the value of information 'to the penny' using such measures, we do advocate using hard measures as much as possible. For example, the amount of time staff spend using information arising from the initiative can be measured and indicates the value those staff place on that information.

Risks and rewards of information management

A risk/reward categorisation of the value of information is shown below, in figure 3.1. Knowledge is enhanced through:

- *Structural* work where obvious information is enhanced: for example, management information systems such as finance, fundraising systems, operational systems for service provision.
- Filling in *uncertain* areas where patterns need to be challenged and anomalies become paramount, for example information that enables practice learning for enhancing and revising service practice.
- Repairing *dangerous* areas of poor knowledge or gaps: for example, donor information and analysis, market research of beneficiary perceptions, regulatory futures.
- *Strategic* information, where thought and consideration are foremost in deriving value from existing information that has not yet brought value.

In the stable state, organisations find patterns of success and reinforce them. Information needs in such circumstances are probably stable and therefore have low marginal cost. Regular financial management information might fall into this category.

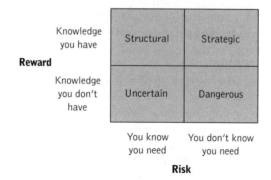

FIGURE 3.1 Risk/reward categories for information and knowledge

In the change state, anomalies indicate that established patterns are undergoing discontinuous change; the underlying paradigms shift and new patterns of success emerge. Information needs in such circumstances tend to change frequently and therefore have higher marginal cost. The tension between the stable and change states is key – timing is everything. If no effort is expended in enhancing knowledge, the knowledge base is probably of little value – an asset without anyone prepared to pay for maintenance is either eternal (e.g. a definition of your cause) or valueless (e.g. an incomplete slightly out of date list of health centres).

The next chapter goes into more detail on how to scope, manage and value knowledge management initiatives.

Summary

- The distinction between information systems and IT infrastructure is important, to enable us to determine who owns, pays for and co-ordinates the various components of our systems.
- Make sure you are clear on who owns, pays for and co-ordinates each aspect of your IT.
- For most organisations there are grey areas where it is difficult to determine who should look after what – the purpose of thinking about these matters is to have clear responsibilities for costs and benefits.
- Depending on the size of your organisation and the complexity of its structure, you should establish appropriate management structures for the ownership, cost-allocation and co-ordination of information systems and IT infrastructure.
- Not-for-profit organisations should feel bound to try to value the benefits of IT, rather than the alternative, which is to spend the organisation's funds on IT in the vague hope that this IT spending will somehow advance the organisation's objectives.
- Use evidential methods borrowed from the world of audit (despite the surreal moniker COD-VERB).
- Where possible, use basic economics ('competitive' pricing theory, marginal costs and marginal revenues) to help you to value your use of IT.

Knowledge management

CHAPTER OBJECTIVES

In this chapter we shall:

- Try to define knowledge management.
- Explain why knowledge management initiatives tend to be difficult to get off the ground and then often drift once they do.
- Provide some useful tips and pointers for successful knowledge management initiatives.
- Illustrate the thinking.

What is knowledge management?

'Knowledge management' is currently a fashionable organisational term. The potential rewards are enormous: cultural cohesion, harnessing know how, sharing skills and experiences, getting tangible gain from your intellectual capital – the list is nearly endless.

As a result, providers of a myriad of products and services are rushing to describe their wares as 'knowledge management'. This variety of claimants includes, but is not restricted to, software producers, change management consultancies, operational process managers, marketing and communications advisors, information technology managers, business strategists and human resources practitioners. Many such claims have validity. While it might be fun to watch internal and external providers competing for the 'knowledge high ground', the diversity generates some practical issues and risks for not-for-profit organisations that actually want to get things done, especially in terms of the definition and ownership of initiatives.

One can sympathise up to a point with organisations struggling to define their knowledge management initiatives. After all, many such initiatives are born from a desire to 'find out what knowledge we have out there' or to 'break down traditional barriers (e.g. regional, departmental) which prevent us from sharing our knowledge'. For example, a large research and development organisation, which described the establishment of its corporate intranet as a knowledge management initiative, was disappointed when the initiative failed to take off. The problem was not the medium (intranets are often very effective media for knowledge management initiatives) but the message (there was little or no guidance to staff on what to do with the medium). This 'initiative' was adrift more or less from the moment it started.

Contrast the above example with a distribution client of ours that established its knowledge management initiative, also using an intranet, around a handful of well defined areas (skills and experience logging, team performance, bulletins and discussion around other initiatives) and provided incentives for timely and accurate update of the information. The company's initiative took off at breakneck speed and the value of the knowledge generated on its corporate intranet is enormous.

Knowledge management initiatives, like all projects, benefit enormously from having a clearly defined scope and objectives. Successful initiatives will of course 'morph' and expand through demand, but that expansion should also be clearly defined and should have tangible objectives.

Managing expectations

Knowledge management initiatives often deliver significant benefits yet fail to meet expectations. Often this is because the initiative was 'sold' (internally or externally) as a panacea and couldn't possibly succeed in meeting the expectations the launch generated. There are several risks arising from unrealistic expectations. Perceived failure despite material successes is a substantial risk. Perhaps more severe (e.g. costly and time wasting) is the risk that the initiative becomes over-engineered in a futile attempt to meet unrealistic expectations.

Ownership of knowledge management initiatives

Most departments or divisions in a sizeable organisation can stake their claim to knowledge management. 'Knowledge management is all about: [information technology], [human resources],

CASE EXAMPLE   A result of unrealistic expectations

A large international not-for-profit organisation asked the current authors to review its knowledge management initiative and explain why it was failing to meet almost everyone's expectations. The programme of work had been 'sold' to staff as a tool kit to help them to manage just about everything the organisation did. In order to try and meet this unrealistic goal, the initiative team had tried to tag on all manner of functions. This organisation had even written its own mini spreadsheet for costing its specific projects and its own mini project management tool for managing its programme of good works. Needless to say, these 'knowledge management

initiative' modules fell short of expectations, were less effective (and much more expensive) than standard software packages and had little (if anything) to do with sharing information and knowledge.

Painful though it might have seemed to this organisation, the sensible way forward was to scale back the scope of the initiative to the core (which was useful, valuable and achievable). This approach enabled the organisation to deliver real benefit to its staff and stakeholders through a scaled down system that people could understand and use easily. The benefits from information and knowledge sharing could then flow.

[strategy and planning], [service delivery], [fundraising], [communications] (delete where inapplicable)'. When initiatives are well defined and clearly focused wholly or primarily in one area, clarity regarding ownership of the initiative is relatively easy to achieve. Where initiatives manifestly cut across existing organisational boundaries (often harder to define but often more effective than departmental initiatives), clarity of ownership can be harder. Many larger organisations, seeing knowledge management as increasingly important and 'boundary shifting', have established knowledge directorates specifically to own and drive their knowledge management initiatives. Others govern their knowledge management initiatives through cross-departmental boards and/or expert panels (this form of ownership is especially common in cross-organisational knowledge management initiatives).

There are no right and wrong answers here. The distribution company referred to above, which focused its first knowledge management initiative on skills and performance, drove the initiative through its human resources function. The less focused R&D organisation at first ran its initiative out of the information technology department. There is an important distinction which frequently gets missed; the distinction between ownership of knowledge management initiatives, ownership of the information within knowledge management initiatives and ownership of the infrastructure (often technological) through which the information is delivered. Each aspect requires clarity of ownership and co-ordination. The thinking here is analogous with the thinking in chapter 3.

Measuring success

Even when the initiative is well defined, expectations are reasonable and ownership of various aspects of the initiative clearly set out, it is often still fiendishly hard to set tangible success measures. Where success is largely intangible and hard to measure there are two polar views: 'don't bother' or 'try harder'. The authors subscribe (within reason) to the latter.

As a minimum, it should be possible to set tangible milestones on the initiative itself and measure whether the activities of the initiative are being achieved on time and on budget without reducing scope. It is usually easy to set some targets and measure information volumes and usage statistics. Such output measures don't necessarily reflect effectiveness, but some measurement is much better than none. Further, in environments where usage is not compulsory or necessary, usage statistics reflect a form of market forces, which is surely at least an indirect measure of effectiveness. If staff are voluntarily 'hitting' the knowledge management system on average eight times a day (as in the case of the distribution company), staff must feel that this is a valuable source for their work. To be sure, usage is only one factor – some elements will be little used but highly effective and valuable while other elements will be used often but add little.

Further, it is always possible to measure perceived value and satisfaction amongst the people involved in the knowledge management initiative, both providers (the initiative team) and users. Successful knowledge management initiatives often emerge from iterative processes. Structured feedback should provide tangible measures over time and provide vital input into the process of continuously improving the knowledge management initiative to minimise the risks and maximise the rewards.

The following table sets out ten top tips for minimising the risks and maximising the rewards from knowledge management initiatives.

TABLE 4.1 Ten tips for achieving success with knowledge management initiatives

Aspect	Risks to minimise/rewards to maximise	Tips
Definition	*Risks* – drifting initiative, unclear scope *Rewards* – achieve valuable objectives	1 Clearly define objectives and scope 2 Use bite-sized chunks to pilot and prove concept 3 Redefine regularly as the initiative expands and changes
Expectations	*Risks* – perceived failure, over-engineered solutions *Rewards* – satisfied constituents	4 Promise only aspects you know can be delivered 5 Gauge demand and prioritise wants and needs
Ownership	*Risks* – lack of leadership, uncontrolled and unreliable information *Rewards* – contribution, consensus and commitment from constituents	6 Distinguish between ownership of the initiative, ownership of information and ownership of the delivery media 7 Clarify and communicate ownership of each aspect
Measuring success	*Risks* – not knowing whether you have succeeded *Rewards* – demonstrable success, platform for improvement	8 If it's hard to measure, try harder 9 Keep constituents informed about successes and failures 10 Seek feedback from constituents to enable you to improve continuously

Summary

- Almost anything and everything might be labelled as knowledge management these days, so ensure that there is clear and sensible scope and well defined objectives to your knowledge management initiative.
- Don't promise more than you can deliver and clarify who owns the knowledge management initiative.
- Ensure that you are measuring the success of the initiative, partly to justify your use of resources and partly to ensure that you are continuously improving your knowledge management.

Part 2

IT structure

IT structure – using this part

This part aims to cover what you might want and need to know about: the kit that contributes to your IT, protecting your investment in IT and complying with good practice, legislation and regulation. You may choose not to read the first chapter – 'The history of IT' – but we hope it is interesting, fun and provides a useful context for much else in the book.

People from most not-for-profit organisations should familiarise themselves with almost all of the material in this part, although the level of detail you will need on the good practice, legislation and regulation will vary with your organisation's size and complexity. We have tried to tailor our advice to enable not-for-profit organisations of all sizes to apply the requirements sensibly.

People from very small organisations, i.e. those which have not connected computers with each other or the outside world, probably don't need to worry too much about chapter 10 – 'Information security'. However, as soon as you do start connecting, then issues raised in that chapter will become pertinent.

The history of IT

CHAPTER OBJECTIVES

In this chapter we shall:

- Sketch the history of IT, focusing on some of the people who initiated the IT revolution.
- Urge you to avoid worrying about the physics and electronics involved unless you are really keen on those subjects.
- Set the history of IT in context for not-for-profit organisations.

A 'one minute history of IT'

Computers have been around for longer than most people realise. The abacus, the comptometer, the electronic typewriter and the punchcard are all examples of devices used for automating aspects of work. For those who are interested in the history of science and technology, the history of computing is especially relevant and there are many books on the subject (see Appendix B – Directory).

For those who have little or no interest in such matters, it is possible to become an expert superuser of IT without ever having heard of, for example:

- Charles Babbage, the nineteenth century visionary who designed (and to some extent built) a prototype computational machine amazingly close in concept to modern computer design but years before it was practical to produce useful devices. Babbage was ably assisted by Countess Ada Lovelace, Lord Byron's daughter. Indeed Ada was probably the uncredited brains behind much of this innovation.

- Alan Turing, whose diverse pioneering work on computer theory in the 1940s and 50s was so exhaustive it still inspires further innovation today. Turing's achievements also included cryptography (code making and breaking): the breaking of the Enigma Code during the Second World War led to the early development of computers (much like those we use today) and probably shortened the war by months or even years.
- William Shockley, whose lead role in the invention of the transistor enabled not only our modern radio and television sets but also the miniaturisation of computing. Prior to the transistor, computers (like radios and televisions) used thermionic valves. Early computers needed thousands of these valves, which made them enormous, hot and inordinately expensive to build and maintain.
- Gordon Moore, whose Intel corporation has consistently dominated the market for microprocessors, which are the main components of computers, for the last twenty years or so. Microprocessors are basically chips of silicon engraved in such a way that they comprise thousands, millions or billions of transistors. In the 1960s, Gordon Moore estimated that advances in silicon chip technologies would enable the world of computing to double the power and halve the unit cost of computing once every eighteen months or so. This rule of thumb, now known as Moore's Law, remarkably has held true for thirty to forty years, should hold true for a further five to ten years and might continue to hold true for longer.
- Bill Gates, whose Microsoft Corporation has dominated the market for operating systems (the intermediary software that enables the machine to communicate with the user software) for about two decades and the market for office tools for about a decade. As a result, Mr Gates is now one of the richest men in the world, although the US anti-trust authorities are having a long look at Microsoft.

Do I need to understand any of the physics and electronics stuff?

No. For the ordinary IT user, the underlying physics and electronics (alluded to above) is even less essential context than the history. The transistors etched on to the silicon chip are essentially a huge collection of on/off switches. Computer programs simply utilise and interpret the output of those switches, using binary (1s and 0s) as the base of calculation to do useful things. By doing many simple calculations very quickly indeed, and by channelling the power of those calculations in useful ways, computers can be made to perform tasks that are helpful and useful to you. Computers really are simply sophisticated calculators configured to do what you recognise as 'the things we use computers to do'.

As the physics and electronics boffins get better and better at channelling computational power, the possibilities for making computers friendlier and more useful to you increase. Until a few years ago, for example, most of us would have been unable to afford sufficient computing power to have Windows images on our screens or speech recognition routines. Today such tools are affordable to most of us. You do not need to understand the complex science that lies behind the advances in information technology, but should be aware of Moore's Law (see above).

Historical context for not-for-profit organisations

Not-for-profit organisations tend to think of themselves as followers rather than leaders in the use of IT. Interestingly enough, though, one of the very first implementations of a large-scale computer system was in a not-for-profit context. Herman Hollerith designed and built a computational machine for the US Census Office to use for the 1890 census. Many experts consider this to be the first practical example of a computer implementation (Babbage's 'machine' never worked). There was much criticism at the time, as the census cost some $11.5 million, double the cost of the previous (unautomated) census. However, experts countered that the cost of the 1890 census would have been much higher without automation and that the use of automation had in fact saved some $5 million.

The not-for-profit sector took very much a back seat in the history of IT after the heady Hollerith days, ceding the centre stage to big business, defence and space exploration (arguably not-for-profit, perhaps) until relatively recently. By the 1960s and 1970s, many larger businesses were using IT for back office tasks such as payroll and financial ledgers. A few larger not-for-profit organisations similarly started to use IT in this way, often through bureau services. Some bureau providers spotted specific opportunities for business in the not-for-profit sector, such as providing donor recording systems to help with fundraising or membership systems for membership-based not-for-profit organisations.

In the 1980s two things started to happen concurrently which started to bring IT into the spotlight for not-for-profit organisations:

■ The sector started to grow substantially and the bigger charities started to become yet larger and more corporate in their approach.

- Computing started to become economically viable for smaller and medium-sized enterprises (SMEs) for the first time, initially with the advent of minicomputers and especially with the advent of personal computing (e.g. the PET, the BBC Acorn/Micro and, in 1981, the IBM-PC) and PC networks.

As with SMEs, not-for-profit organisations tended to focus at first on administrative functions such as accounting and payroll, plus donor and membership records. Specialist voluntary sector oriented suppliers emerged, many of whom tried to cover many aspects of administration, not just the voluntary sector bits. Many not-for-profit organisations struggled long and hard with ghastly financial systems which 'came as part of the suite' with the donor recording system they wanted and there were still many not-for-profit organisations using bureau services well into the 1990s. Some organisations are still struggling along with ghastly old ledgers and the like, although the imperative to upgrade to avoid Year 2000 (Y2K) problems drove out many of the old dinosaur applications in the late 1990s.

Strangely, the advent of application service providers (ASPs – see chapter 3) in the commercial sector has raised the notion once again that an approach very similar to the bureau style (using a third party to look after your computing and application needs), once so popular with the not-for-profit sector, might be back in fashion. This time around, it might be smaller organisations that take the lead with the ASP model. This interesting area of development is discussed, in context, in several chapters of this book.

Fad and fashions come and go in the IT sector. Nevertheless, it is clear that IT has relentlessly invaded the not-for-profit sector since the 1980s and is without question here to stay for all but the smallest organisations.

Summary

- You do not really need to understand the history of IT to be able to enjoy the benefits of IT, but it is fun, interesting and useful context.
- You do not really need to understand the physics and electronics (although it is also fun and interesting), but it does help if you appreciate that the progress scientists are making looks set to continue to improve price/performance of IT for many years to come.
- Not-for-profit organisations don't tend to do groundbreaking things with IT, although the sector can boast the first genuinely practical IT implementation in the form of the Hollerith US census of 1890.
- Fads and fashions come and go, but since the 1980s IT has relentlessly invaded the not-for-profit sector and is here to stay.

Machines: on your desk and in networks

CHAPTER OBJECTIVES

In this chapter we shall:

- Remind you that you do not really need to know very much about the equipment on your desk.
- Explain a little about the equipment.
- Explain a little about forms of computer networking you are likely to come across, from small local networks to the internet.
- Provide definitions, diagrams and analogies which might help when technical people riddle you with jargon.

Don't let the jargon vendors get to you

As a user of information technology, you need to know very little about the equipment you use. You do need to understand what you are using it for, but not the details of how the machines work or the underlying physics and electronics. Strangely, computer vendors too often focus sales pitches on the technical functions, gadgets and gizmos, leaving mere mortals like us perplexed.

Today, most people take it for granted that their hi-fi equipment has complex electronic circuitry inside that they do not need to understand as an ordinary listener. We are simply listeners. Avid users of IT can similarly distance themselves from the kit.

The following table sets out analogous categories of hi-fi buffs and IT people. The vast majority of us fall into the last category.

TABLE 6.1 Different types of users

Type of user	Known as in information technology circles	Known as in hi-fi circles
Manufacturer/repairer	Electrical/electronic engineer	Electrical/electronic engineer
Technical enthusiast	Geek, propeller-head, IT hobbyist	Boffin, DIY enthusiast
Professional user	Software engineer, IT support, 'superuser'	Disc jockey, sound engineer
Most of us	Users	Listeners

A little bit on equipment that might help a lot

The figures below illustrate a typical computer user's desktop from the device viewpoint and function viewpoint respectively.

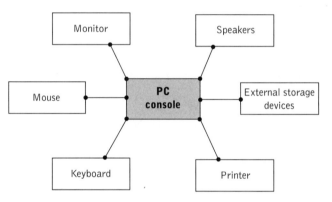

FIGURE 6.1 Typical computer from a 'device' viewpoint

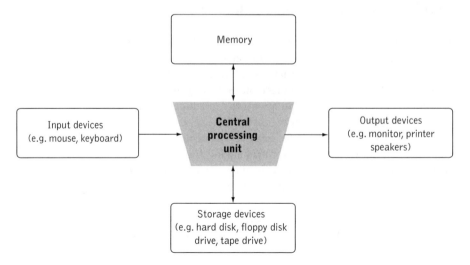

FIGURE 6.2 Typical computer from a 'function' viewpoint

TABLE 6.2 Desktop equipment explained

Term	Alternative terms	Explanation	Musical analogy
Computer	Personal computer, PC, Mac, desktop computer, microcomputer, display screen equipment	A programmable electronic device used for processing data, calculations etc.	The whole musical instrument
Monitor	Visual display unit (VDU), screen	Device on which a computer displays information	The music stand
Central processing unit	CPU, console, system unit, terminal	The main part of the computer, containing the processor and to which most other parts of the computer connect	The part of the musical instrument that causes the sound
Keyboard	None commonly used	An input device, similar to a typewriter keyboard	A part of the musical instrument that you use to operate the instrument
Mouse	None commonly used	An input device, commonly used to control a pointer on the computer screen	A part of the musical instrument that you use to operate the instrument
Speakers	None commonly used	An output device for sound, often coming in twos owing to popularity of stereo sound	The same devices are used in amplified music
External storage devices	Hard disk drives, floppy disk drives, tape drives, ZIP drives, JAZZ drives	A device outside the CPU used for storing data. Modern machines tend to have substantial storage devices (mostly hard disks) within the machine	Cassette recorders, minidisk machines, video recorders, DVDs
Printer	None commonly used	An output device for producing printed text or graphics	A part of the musical instrument that transmits the sound

In order to help those readers who are less familiar with the buzz words and jargon, we have attempted in the table above to explain the most commonly used terms by analogy with the world of music.

Computer networks

Most organisations use some form of networking nowadays. A 1999 survey, *Information and communications technology: Reshaping the voluntary sector*, (Burt and Taylor, 1999) identified that:

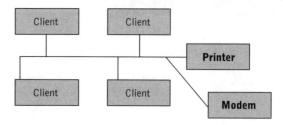

FIGURE 6.3 Peer to peer network

- Eighty-four per cent of not-for-profit organisations use 'some form of networking'.
- Fifty-seven per cent of not-for-profit organisations declared themselves to be 'more than 50 per cent networked' and 80 per cent planned to be so.
- Thirty-five per cent of not-for-profit organisations use 'some remote working' and 62 per cent planned to do so.
- There was little correlation between size of not-for-profit organisation and the take-up of networking technologies.

Local area networking

A local area network (LAN) is a network of several computers restricted to a single room or building. They come in two main forms:

- Peer to peer networks (suitable for connecting a handful of devices – see figure 6.3).
- Client-server networks (suitable for connecting several hundred devices – see figure 6.4).

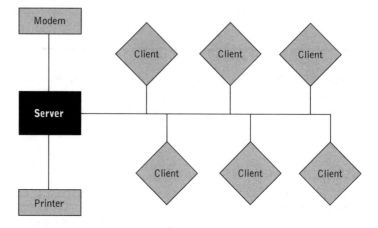

FIGURE 6.4 Client-server network – thick client technologies

Local area networking does have its technical issues, but smaller organisations can usually navigate these with minimal fuss as long as their vendor is trustworthy and sensible. Items to look out for include:

- Choice of network operating system (if starting today, normally Windows NT or possibly Novell).
- Type of cabling to choose (Category 5 or above is highly recommended if starting or recabling today).
- Whether to combine voice and data in the cabling (if starting today the answer is usually yes).

Wide area networking

Organisations that operate over a distributed geographical area might use a wide area network (WAN). These come in several forms, including:

1 Private network using leased lines (e.g. BT kilostream).
2 Value-added dedicated network (e.g. Cable & Wireless frame relay).
3 Virtual private network (VPN – not dedicated but with guaranteed availability).
4 Public network – e.g. 'virtual' WAN service through your internet service provider, using the internet (or world wide web) as the communication channel.
5 Dial-up connection, which itself comes in several forms, including:
   - ISDN – integrated services digital network (e.g. BT Highway)
   - PSTN – public switch telephone network (most conventional telephone services)
   - ADSL – asymmetric digital subscriber line (starting to become available at the time of writing and showing promise as a cost effective form once widely available).

Dedicated WANs (1 and 2 above) are normally more secure, reliable and expandable. Virtual WANs (3 and 4 above) are cheaper, flexible and easy to use. Dial-up WAN connections are usually sensible for occasional users but tend to become very expensive on phone call charges if those occasional users become more regular.

There is a host of technical issues to think about when choosing WAN options, which can have significant cost and practical implications, even for small organisations implementing small WANs. If you do not have access to someone with genuine experience and expertise in this area, it normally pays to get some professional advice before you commit to a WAN. Aspects you need to consider include:

- The applications people want to use across the WAN.
- The configuration of WAN you choose from the above list (this might well include a mixture of methods depending on geography, usage and budget).
- Whether some or all of the applications might be hosted by an applications service provider (ASP – see chapter 3) rather than hosted on your organisation's servers.
- Anticipated usage, demand loading, peak times, geographical diversity and how usage might change once you get up and running.
- The capacity of the connection required (also known as bandwidth requirement).
- The processing and communication technology used for the chosen applications across the WAN, which might include:
  - conventional client-server computing, also known as 'thick client' technologies, in which lots of data moves up and down the line (see figure 6.4, above).
  - 'thin' client technologies, e.g. Citrix Metaframe or Microsoft Terminal Server, which makes the client machine act a bit like a 'Windows dumb terminal' and almost all the work takes place on the servers in the centre, requiring much less data to move up and down the line (see figure 6.5, below).

Below are some lessons and golden rules for wide area networking:

- Specify what you need before you buy.
- Try to think ahead more than spend ahead.
- Don't be afraid to mix and match technologies – most people need to do this to some extent these days to achieve what they want at the right price.

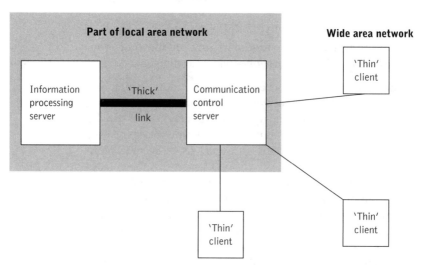

FIGURE 6.5 Thin client topology

TABLE 6.3 Networking explained

Term	Alternative terms	Explanation	Musical analogy
Server	SuperPC, fileserver, central PC, main PC	A computer whose task is primarily or exclusively to run the network	Leader of the band, conductor of the orchestra
Peer to peer network	Small-scale local area network (LAN), serverless network – see figure 6.3	A method of file sharing in which computers are linked to each other	Perhaps a pop group, perhaps a duo, trio, quartet or quintet (above that size is pushing it), with no conductor
Client-server network	Local area network (LAN), full-scale or 'proper' computer network – see figure 6.4	A method of file sharing in which the users' computers (clients) share files through a central computer (server)	An orchestra, in which the artists are the clients and the conductor is the server
Wide area network (WAN)	None commonly used	A network that connects computers distributed over a wide geographical area	Perhaps Barbara Streisand and Donna Summer recording a duet on opposite sides of the US; perhaps a recording studio with parts of the orchestra located at different sites
The internet	The net	Global computer network embracing electronic mail, electronic bulletin boards, sending and retrieving files, conferencing, chat services and information exchange	Might be thought of as broadcasting, recording, distribution of recordings, concerts and 'jam sessions' all rolled into one
World wide web	The web, WWW, W3	A graphical system (using hypertext) for publishing and accessing information on the internet	Perhaps the equivalent of Classic FM, the Sony Walkman, CDs and 'in the park' concerts rolled into one

- Ensure that you put appropriate levels of security in place for the data involved (see 'Data protection', chapter 11).
- Make sure that your policies and procedures, not just your technology, are secure.
- Enjoy the benefits of networking.

The benefits of wide area networking for not-for-profit organisations include:

- 'Virtually' bringing remote workers such as field fundraisers, volunteers and local projects into the fold.

- Decentralisation of processing and/or access to information such as finance, fundraising data or grant applications information.
- Enabling more flexible working, such as home working or peripatetic workers connecting from various sites of activity.
- Increased timeliness and efficiency of information exchange, such as field reports, expenses, document collaboration.

Continuing the musical analogy

We've introduced a great many terms and definitions in this chapter. It's pretty much impossible to talk about networking without introducing these terms. In order to soften the blow, we've tried our best in table 6.3 (page 51) to extend the musical analogy we used in figure 6.2.

Summary

- You really do not need to know much about the equipment you use, but some people are enthusiastic about such matters.
- We have used hi-fi and music as an analogy to help you to understand key terms. As IT equipment becomes more commoditised, our attitude towards the equipment is likely to become more like our attitude to domestic equipment – we'll neither know nor care much about what goes on inside the box.
- You are increasingly likely to come across networking of some sort in your organisation.
- Local area networking is a fairly well ploughed furrow these days, although larger networks do need a fair amount of ongoing support.
- There's a lot to think about when wide area networking as the costs and potential benefits can be very high in relation to your organisation's size – so don't be afraid to seek professional advice where appropriate.

Operating systems, utilities, virus avoidance

CHAPTER OBJECTIVES

In this chapter we shall:

- Outline what operating systems are.
- Give a little information about a useful class of software known as utilities.
- Discuss software viruses and some tips on how to avoid them as best you can.

Operating systems

A computer's operating system is the software that acts as an intermediary, enabling the user and the user's application software to communicate with the machine. See figure 7.1, overleaf.

Most PCs today use a version of Microsoft Windows as the operating system. Prior to that most PCs used DOS as their operating system. (Sorry Mac users, but the numbers are overwhelming.) Examples of operating systems you might come across at an organisational level (e.g. to run servers and networks) are Novell, Unix, Linux and Windows NT.

It could be argued that web browsers (e.g. Internet Explorer, Netscape, Mosaic) are forms of operating system. Some simple machines (e.g. prototype Network Computers – NCs) can run application software across the internet using web browsers alone. At the time of writing, this approach to computing does not appear to be a viable alternative to conventional computing for most organisations. However, the threat posed by web browsers as an alternative to the ubiquitous Windows has formed a key part of the Microsoft anti-trust legal action in the US.

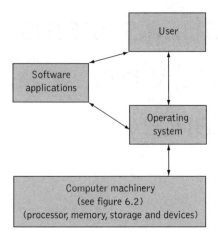

FIGURE 7.1 The operating system protects you (the user) from the computer 'machinery'

Utilities

There is another category of structural software known as utilities. These are useful small packages that tend to do things you wish your operating system could do. Examples include Lotus Screencam for recording the animation of your screens for later viewing, McAfee First Aid for finding out why your computer is going wrong, Quarterdeck QEMM for improving the memory capability of your PC, Symantec pcAnywhere for remote access, conversion programs; the list could go on and on.

Virus protection

If you only splash out on one utility package, it should probably be anti-virus protection. The main products are McAfee, Norton and Dr Solomons, all of which offer subscriptions to keep your protection up to date and most of which will throw in some other utilities and/or bundled deals if you buy several licences. Computer viruses are more than just a nuisance, they threaten the safety of your information, as well as having the potential to cause you inordinate stress, cost, effort and embarrassment. Anti-virus software does not guarantee that you won't fall victim to a computer virus, but adequate software protection together with sensible policies and procedures for avoiding receiving viruses in the first place minimise the risk.

Those sensible policies and procedures for virus avoidance should include:

- Regularly updating your anti-virus software as new viruses are being created all the time. The better anti-virus packages make it easy for you to update regularly, e.g. through the internet.
- Virus checking incoming floppy disks, CDs, etc. before loading them on to your PC.
- Not booting your machine from a floppy disk unless the disk is a write-protected boot disk specifically for that purpose.
- Virus checking incoming word processing, spreadsheet, presentation and database files, even if they appear to come from reliable sources. Be especially vigilant if they come from unexpected sources.
- Being especially vigilant about file attachments that come with e-mails as many viruses are spread this way. At the time of writing, plain e-mails cannot contain viruses themselves and you need to load an attached file in order to get infected. There are rumours afoot that plain e-mails might soon become a risk.
- Not using pirate software or supplying copies of your software illegally to other people.
- Trying to keep a specific PC off the network (often referred to as a 'dirty PC') for testing files if the nature of your work requires you to work with files of doubtful origin.

If you are nevertheless unfortunate enough to get (or believe you have) a virus on your PC, take the following sensible steps:

- Do not panic – often the worst damage done as a result of the virus is the user destroying things while trying to resolve the problem. There is also a class of pest known as hoax viruses, for example e-mails which tell you have a virus and encourage you to spread the word and do daft things. This is one time when you should seek advice rather than tinker in the hope of self-sufficiency.
- Do not follow on-screen instructions which might be coming from the virus – these are often bogus and might be encouraging you to do damage that the inventor of the virus was unable or unwilling to automate.
- Do not let anyone else use your PC until the problem is completely solved.
- Isolate all media (e.g. floppy disks) that you might have used on your machine since infection and do not let anyone use those media until they have been checked and 'disinfected'.
- Make sure that someone who is sufficiently expert and experienced ensures that the virus really is cleared.
- Alert your colleagues and anyone else you suspect you might have been infected. It is embarrassing to pass on a software virus but it is even worse to exacerbate the problem by failing to come clean about it.

Summary

- The operating system is software that enables the user and the user's application software to communicate with the machine.
- Utilities are dull but useful 'housekeeping' software applications, often things that you wished your operating system could do.
- Software viruses are a risk to all organisations using computers, but the use of anti-virus utilities and sensible procedures should make the risk of infection quite small.

Maintenance, support, facilities management

CHAPTER OBJECTIVES

In this chapter we shall:

- Sketch out the basics on warranties, maintenance and support.
- Probably make you feel a bit better about your maintenance and support problems by telling you that you are not alone.
- Provide some thoughts on how to get the most out of your maintenance and support provider, including some considerations on self sufficiency and/or using a third party to manage your IT facility.

Warranties

Most machines come with warranties (usually one, two or three years) which can be 'on-site' (the supplier will come to you) or 'return to base' (you have to send the machine back to the supplier). It is always worth checking at the procurement stage the duration and type of warranties you are buying, especially if you are price shopping, as the difference in price between machines can sometimes be attributable to a difference in warranty provision.

Maintenance and support

Regardless of warranties, most charities use (or wish to use) a third party for the maintenance and support of the structural element of their IT (machines and operating systems). It is easier to find suppliers if you are a very big charity – as large engineering and IT facilities management companies are probably going to be interested in the top fifty to a hundred charities – or a very small charity, as local high street IT shops (probably the source of your equipment) often provide a good personal service to single site charities.

For those in between, say charities with five to fifty machines and possibly more than one site, it frequently seems to be problem getting a suitably qualified and located support company sufficiently interested. Perseverance will usually pay off in the end and it is better to keep shopping around than to put up with dreadful service. If you get dark days you can console yourself by remembering that standards of service in this area of IT are generally pretty low throughout the UK. In other words you are probably no worse off than most of your peers.

It is important that your maintenance and support contract is clear about service levels, such as call-out lead time (usually four working hours or eight working hours, the latter being significantly cheaper) and which aspects of your computing are covered by the agreement. Make sure that the supplier is aware of machines that are still under warranty, as this should have an impact on the price of your maintenance contract. It is also important for you to clarify which aspects are covered by your regular fee and which aspects you will pay for 'as-you-go'. When you do have an element of 'pay-as-you-go', ascertain when the clock starts ticking (e.g. are you paying for travel?) and whether you have to cover travelling expenses. If you have any sites in remote places these aspects can have serious cost implications. When asking for quotes, ask suppliers to offer you a choice of service levels and alternative mixes of fixed fee and 'pay-as-you-go', so you can choose an arrangement most suited to your budget and your needs.

If you are able, it helps to have an element of self-sufficiency with regard to support. That doesn't mean a screwdriver and soldering iron for the chief executive, but it does mean, for example:

- Having a spare 'standby' machine available and ready, if you are able to do so. Although this might seem wasteful, it can often be cheaper and more effective to have extended return to base warranties with a standby machine, than to have expensive on-site support contracts with a poor service provider.
- Designating one or more members of staff to co-ordinate and gate-keep support issues.
- If you can manage the budgetary risk, being prepared to have a policy of 'chuck and replace' for older equipment, rather than deferring the inevitable cost of replacement, possibly with relatively expensive maintenance.

If your organisation is large enough to have one or more dedicated IT staff, you should consider using a third party to manage the facility comprehensively, for example to provide full support of networks, desktop PCs, operating systems and office applications. This approach can make sense financially, especially in circumstances where a commercial facilities manager can achieve economies of scale on your behalf. Although a relatively unusual approach for not-for-profits at the moment, managed IT facilities are increasingly popular for smaller and medium sized enterprises. It is increasingly common for maintenance and support companies to offer wider IT facilities services.

You should ask potential providers of maintenance and support for their ideas on managing the whole IT facility. Such ideas can also make your organisation look more attractive to providers, encouraging them to engage in discussions with you whereas they might not otherwise be interested in your organisation. Even if you decide to choose a traditional maintenance and support contract for the time being, obtaining estimates for a comprehensive managed service can help you to gauge whether you are getting reasonable value for money from your current IT support provision.

There is further discussion about outsourcing aspects of your organisation's IT service in chapter 19.

Summary

- Warranties are a significant part of the cost of equipment, so you should be aware of them and take advantage of them where you can.
- Most not-for-profit organisations will use a third party for maintenance and support to some extent – few express delight at the service they receive.
- Try to make the best of a bad job through being sensibly self sufficient and/or considering using a third party provider you like and trust to look after your IT facilities in a comprehensive way.

Avoiding and preparing for the worst

CHAPTER OBJECTIVES

In this chapter we shall:

- Provide you with some tips on insuring your equipment.
- Set out some basic guidelines, checklists and templates to help you with the physical security of your systems.
- Scare you into backing up your data, including giving pragmatic advice on taking back ups and ensuring that they are effective.
- Discuss IT catastrophes and related subjects.
- Help you to think through some of the issues involved in trying to ensure that your organisation's show stays on the road even if the worst does happen.

Insurance

You will normally insure your office-based computer equipment under your standard office policies. You might choose to have cover for consequential loss (e.g. loss of revenue in the event of business interruption or high value data loss). Your insurance company is likely to have rules and exclusions for higher value items. Normally, insurance company stipulations are common sense, minimum requirements, such as:

- Security marking devices.
- Physically lock-securing devices (e.g. in a cage or cabinet).
- Restricted physical access to key equipment.
- Electrical spike protection and uninterruptable power supply to key devices.

- Appropriate back up devices and policies for their use (regularity, off-site storage procedure) to minimise the risk of high value data loss and/or lengthy business interruption (see below).

If you are using portable computers (laptops, palmtops, hand-held computers etc.) you will also need some form of 'all risks' policy to ensure that the equipment is covered away from your premises. It often makes sense to have the all risks policy separate from your office policy, to ensure that your claims record on one does not taint your claims record on the other type. In any event, at the time of writing it is nigh on impossible to get any insurer to cover portable computing devices in certain circumstances. Our advice with regard to portable computers is therefore – do not leave portable computing devices unattended in:

- An unlocked place.
- A locked place if the device is visible to passers by (e.g. through a window or glass door).
- A motor vehicle, even if the vehicle is locked and the device is not visible to passers by (motor insurance won't cover this either).

Physical security

It is part of your trustees' fiduciary duty to ensure that you properly protect the assets of your not-for-profit organisation. It is also a legal requirement under the Data Protection Act (see chapter 11) that you maintain reasonable levels of security for any data you hold.

Strangely, people sometimes put a great deal of effort into having high levels of data (or logical) security and forget about some of the basics for maintaining physical security. Many of the severest and most likely risks to your equipment and the information on it stem from physical security risks. The main categories of risk are:

- Natural disasters such as fire, flood, earthquake, storm damage.
- Failure of or disruption to essential services, such as power cuts.
- Malicious or criminal damage to equipment and/or associated facilities.
- Accidental damage to equipment and/or associated facilities.
- Unauthorised use of equipment.

In order to implement sound physical security procedures, you need to consider the following main questions:

- Do you know exactly what equipment you have and where it is located?

- Have you implemented physical and environmental security measures to protect that equipment?
- Do you have appropriate administrative controls in place to ensure that the physical security of your equipment is maintained?

As always with areas of risk, you need to assess the severity and likelihood of the risks in order to decide the extent to which you should protect yourself. Especially with smaller not-for-profit organisations, these can be tricky decisions. You probably don't have enough time or money to implement all the ideas in the checklist on the next page, but similarly you might not have enough money to replace machines if they are stolen and not insured.

The following table sets out key risk factors for physical security in not-for-profit organisations, which you can use to help you assess the risks you face.

TABLE 9.1 Physical security risk factors

Risk factor	Notes and comments
Is the equipment spread across many different sites?	Each site will have physical security risks of its own
To what extent do you use portable computers?	Portables are especially high risk – see 'Insurance', above
Does the public have easy access to areas where equipment is kept?	Can be especially high risk for some not-for-profit organisations, e.g. a drop-in centre for young people who are in trouble
Is some of the equipment located in places with particular propensities to natural disasters and/or malicious damage?	Not-for-profit organisations often work in places with high risks of natural disasters, political or social upheaval
Is the information on the equipment especially sensitive and/or confidential?	Some not-for-profit organisations handle very high risk information, e.g. a fostering and adoption placement charity. Although logical security should mitigate much of this risk, the existence of that sensitive data within the system also increases the physical security risks
Is the equipment potentially capable of authorising or making financial payments?	Although logical security should mitigate much of this risk, the existence of that capability within the system also increases the physical security risks
Have you had an incident or circumstances that might lead you to believe that a disaffected person or organisation has malicious intent towards your organisation?	Disaffected former staff members are a common example of this risk. In not-for-profit organisations, there are often additional risk factors. For example, equipment in a shelter for survivors of physical abuse might be at physical risk from physical abusers, or a medical research charity's equipment might be at risk from militant animal rights campaigners

You can use the following checklist to help you to manage physical security risks. Check each risk area under the headings 'assessment, impact and mitigation', 'severity' and 'likelihood'. Larger not-for-profit organisations should develop more comprehensive and specific security checklists and procedures, but the following should form a good starting point for any organisation embarking on such an exercise.

PHYSICAL SECURITY CHECKLIST

What you are securing

- ☑ Do you have up to date inventory of all your computer equipment? (see below)
- ☑ Do you have up to date records on the locations of your system documentation?
- ☑ Do you have up to date inventory of all of your software? (see below)
- ☑ Do you have up to date records of your data back up locations?
- ☑ Do you know the location of your disaster recovery plan?

How you are securing it

- ☑ Do you keep the main computers (e.g. servers) in a secure room dedicated to computer equipment?
- ☑ Is access to your main computer room securely restricted to relevant personnel?
- ☑ Is the main computer room located in a relatively environmentally safe place?
- ☑ Is the main computer room protected with fire detectors, smoke detectors and/or fire extinguishers?
- ☑ Do your main computer(s) have a clean power supply, (e.g. special power line or electrical spike removing devices)?
- ☑ Do your main computer(s) have an uninterruptable power supply?
- ☑ Are some computers located in places where the public might have access?
- ☑ Do you security mark the computer equipment?
- ☑ Do you use machine power-up passwords on the computers?
- ☑ Is the equipment physically secured? (e.g. PCs bolted to the desk or housing)
- ☑ Are portable computers locked away out of sight when unattended?
- ☑ Are secure access devices (e.g. bank payment transition devices) kept locked away, accessible only to authorised personnel?

Who is securing it

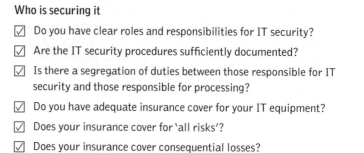

- ☑ Do you have clear roles and responsibilities for IT security?
- ☑ Are the IT security procedures sufficiently documented?
- ☑ Is there a segregation of duties between those responsible for IT security and those responsible for processing?
- ☑ Do you have adequate insurance cover for your IT equipment?
- ☑ Does your insurance cover for 'all risks'?
- ☑ Does your insurance cover consequential losses?

To help you to comply with the checklist you should keep a note of the following:

Basic hardware inventory	**Basic software inventory**
■ Inventory reference number	■ Inventory reference number
■ Date purchased	■ Date purchased
■ Make/model/specification	■ Name of vendor
■ Maker's serial number	■ Author/package/version
■ Cost	■ Licence serial number
■ Location	■ Cost
■ Warranty/maintained by	■ Location
■ Notes	■ Notes

Backing up

It's rather a shame, but this subject tends to make people's eyes glaze over. A shame, because backing up your data properly is one of the most basic and crucial things you can do to protect your investment in IT. Backing up is the process of making a secure copy of your data and/or programs as a contingency in the event that something goes wrong with the original data. Losing data is a significant risk in using IT, but one of the great benefits of using IT is the relative low cost and ease with which secure copies can be made to protect your investment. Consider the following two horror stories.

Backing up – get the basics right

There are a number of major lessons from those two horror stories:

- ■ There is no such thing as 'not having enough budget to be equipped to back up'. If there isn't enough budget for back ups, there isn't enough budget for a computer and/or there isn't enough budget for staff to work on the computer. There is

CASE EXAMPLE   False economy

A good friend telephoned and asked me if we would do her a favour and help her sister who was going frantic. The sister ran a small community-based membership organisation and she was the one full-time worker. The organisation's computer had been stolen in a burglary overnight. Could we help? 'We'll try,' we said, and one of us phoned the sister. 'Everything was on that machine, everything', she said, 'the accounts, the membership records, our community contacts, correspondence going back five years ... '

'We'll lend you a machine to get you up and running again pdq', we said. 'Have they taken your back up device as well. What medium were you using for your back ups?'

'I didn't take back ups. I didn't have enough budget for a back up device when I first got the computer. In the early days I used to copy stuff on to floppy disks, but when the files all got too big for floppies I stopped copying. Please help'. The only help we could manage in those circumstances was to offer our condolences.

CASE EXAMPLE   Flawed back ups

A large and well known campaigning organisation had an IT department with several people, comprehensive back up procedures and an air of confidence even after the new main server crashed and took all the data with it. They had back ups, everything would be OK. Most things were OK and were up and running again within a day. But one key system (used for the administration of a large proportion of the organisation's fundraising income) was not OK. This system had recently been

moved on to the new server, probably in a hurry, and the back ups had not been set up correctly. Worse, even the back ups from the old server (several weeks old, but at least it would have been something) would not restore. No one had ever tested whether the back ups on that old server could actually be restored and used. In fact, for this particular fundraising system, there was a flaw in the back up. Result: misery for many weeks.

simply no point investing money in IT and investing effort in running a system if you are going to put all of that investment at undue risk by not backing up.

■ Make sure you are backing up all of your data files – it is easy to overlook the one system that runs on another machine or the system whose data is stored in a separate partition on your hard drive.

■ Regularly ensure that your back ups are effective by testing that you can restore the system from the back ups. Most of us (if we are lucky) take back ups for years without ever really needing to use them, but you need to know that if you ever did need to use them that they really work. Do not confuse running verification routines (which often come as part of back up software – these are useful but only part of the story) with actually testing your ability to restore.

■ Make sure that you have back ups off site, to mitigate the risk of a physical disaster destroying the back up as well as the main storage. The use of wide area networking and/or application service providers (ASPs – see chapter 3) can help you to achieve practical solutions for off-site back up.

■ Backing up is not fun. But it is an essential risk management practice and almost all of the very worst imaginable IT disasters can be largely avoided if you have backed up properly.

The following checklist should help you to get your back ups right. Again, check each risk area under the headings 'assessment, impact and mitigation', 'severity' and 'likelihood'. Larger not-for-profit organisations should develop more comprehensive and specific back up checklists and procedures, but the following should form a good starting point even for larger organisations.

BACKING UP CHECKLIST

What you are backing up

☑ Do you have up to date inventory of all of your computer equipment? (see page 64)

☑ Do you know where all the programs and data are stored?

☑ Do you know which files you need to back up in order to avoid loss of records and/or losing the ability to function?

How you are backing up

☑ Are you backing up frequently enough?

☑ Do you have appropriate back up devices and media for those devices, e.g. tape, CD, DVD?

☑ Are you logging the back ups?

☑ Is someone checking that you following proper procedures each time you back up?

☑ Do you verify your back ups?

☑ Are some or all of your back ups taken off site?

☑ Are your back ups kept in secure and appropriate places?

☑ Do you periodically test that you are able to recover from your back ups?

Who is backing up and restoring

☑ Do you have clear roles and responsibilities for backing up and restoring?

☑ Are the back up and restore procedures sufficiently documented?

IT business continuity

It is often difficult to separate IT business continuity from general business continuity planning, as many of the catastrophic risks you are trying to mitigate would have an impact on your organisation beyond IT (e.g. a major flood, fire or failure of public services). However, there are catastrophic risks that are IT specific, the most pressing of which (data loss through hardware or software catastrophe) you try to mitigate in part through back ups.

Having back ups, however, is only part of the story, as you need to think through how you would get your show back on the road in the event of various catastrophes. If your office burns down taking all of your machines with it, you might be able to wave the back up tapes around with a smug grin on your face, but you will need some space and machines as well as those tapes to get up and running again.

You might choose to subscribe to a business continuity, disaster recovery or data recovery service, which is in effect an insurance policy of sorts, as you are paying for the ability to use space and/or equipment in the event of a catastrophe. The 'Rolls Royce' form of the service is known as a 'hot site', which is basically a site with equipment that fits your specification, waiting for you to turn up with your back ups so that you can get up and running again almost immediately. A 'cold site' is a suitable site with no equipment in it. A 'warm site' is somewhere in between, where you would probably have the cabling and some equipment in place, with other equipment being procured or swapped in to the site in the event of an emergency.

Some organisations make formal or informal arrangements with other organisations to help each other out in the event of a catastrophe. A collective approach of this sort is welcome, especially in the impecunious not-for-profit sector, but it is important to realise the limitations of such an approach, especially if the arrangement is entirely informal.

Your decision on the extent to which you make prior arrangements will depend on many factors, including:

- The extent to which you are insured for consequential loss.
- The requirements of your insurance policy.
- What you can realistically afford.
- The extent to which you believe you are particularly at risk (e.g. your offices are located in a flood risk zone).
- The loss you think you would actually incur if your operation was down for (e.g. a day, a week, a month, three months).

The important point is that you have a plan and you know how you would deal with the various catastrophic events. You need clear roles and responsibilities for dealing with the disaster and for ensuring IT business continuity after the event. The plan should also cover minimising the risks of catastrophe and (where possible) mitigating any losses arising. You should also test your plan, to satisfy yourselves that it would work if the worst did happen.

IT business continuity planning is not the most fun part of this book but it is important that you consider it. We hope you never have to implement your plan.

Summary

- Make sure you have adequate insurance and that you comply with the requirements of your insurance policy.
- Think about the specific physical security risks that your organisation faces when considering security measures – use the physical security checklist to help you.
- Backing up properly is one of the most effective things you can do to minimise the risk of serious data loss, so make sure you back up regularly and that you test restore from back ups at reasonable intervals.
- Think about the catastrophes that might hit you.
- Within your means and perception of risk, ensure that you have an adequate plan in place to get your show back on the road as quickly and efficiently as possible.

Information security

CHAPTER OBJECTIVES

In this chapter we shall:

- Cover the logical security aspects of information security.
- Explain an holistic model of information security, BS7799, which also encompasses aspects covered in the previous chapter.
- Outline how the information security management standard can help support your work to ensure that your systems are as secure as possible.

Logical security

Although the risks anticipated in chapter 9 are probably the most severe and likely physical risks for not-for-profit organisations, as soon as an organisation connects several computers together or enables access from the outside, it needs also to consider logical security. Logical security is a system of controls and procedures to minimise the risk of an unauthorised person accessing a particular system or data. While physical security might reduce the risk of unauthorised access somewhat, it does not eliminate it. For example, one of your fundraisers might have physical access to the same work space as your payroll clerk, but you can prevent the fundraiser from accessing the payroll through logical security (e.g. password protection on the payroll program and encryption of the payroll data). Logical security is the intangible security that supplements your physical security.

As more and more organisations are 'wired' to the outside world for e-mail, use of the world wide web etc., the risk of unauthorised access through hacking from a remote location increases.

This makes physical security decreasingly important and logical security increasingly important.

Logical security can be provided to any or all of the following aspects of your IT:

- hardware
- operating system
- application system
- data.

It is important that you know at the time you set up your security what you want to protect and why, and how the applications and data are held. This is an area where it is often beneficial to get some expert advice if you are at all unsure. Further, you need to adopt the sneaky mind of an IT hacker to make sure that you really are securing the data. The case example below illustrates this point.

The checklist opposite sets out key risk factors for logical security in not-for-profit organisations, which you can use to help you

---

CASE EXAMPLE   How did they break in to our payroll?

A large not-for-profit organisation client discovered that some disaffected staff had somehow managed to find out several senior managers' salaries. Investigation of manual procedures and interviews with confidential staff led the investigators to believe that the most likely cause was unauthorised access to the payroll data. But how? To access the payroll system, you needed to use two levels of password, which only a handful of confidential staff knew.

However, that particular payroll system had what is sometimes called a 'back door.' It stored data in an unencrypted form on a network drive. We quickly ascertained that the network drive was not logically protected and that theoretically any user could go to that drive and examine the payroll data files. This seemed the most likely source of security breach.

The theory was soon proved, when the local drive of one of the disaffected staff

members was found to contain a copy of a payroll data file and some other files which showed that this person had been extracting information from those files and working out which fields related to people's salaries.

The client commented on this matter, 'I thought we were secure. It wouldn't even have occurred to me to try to break into a system that way'.

The moral of this case study is to:

- ensure that sensitive systems you are procuring protect the data at the same time as they protect the application system (e.g. through encryption or binding the files together), or

- apply additional layers of logical security (e.g. password protected network data drives) to minimise the risk of unauthorised access to data relating to application systems which do not provide sufficient protection in themselves.

assess the risks you face, under the headings 'assessment, impact and mitigation', 'severity' and 'likelihood'.

LOGICAL SECURITY CHECKLIST

What you are securing

- ☑ Do you have an up to date inventory of all your computer systems?
- ☑ Do you have up to date records on the access controls used for each aspect of each system?
- ☑ Have you identified clear responsibilities for administering security for each system?
- ☑ Have you identified specific risk factors for specific systems (e.g. fraud risk for payroll, poaching risk for fundraising data)

Logical hardware security

- ☑ Do you enforce machine power-on passwords for computers?
- ☑ Do you employ additional hardware access controls where appropriate (e.g. swipe cards, BACS code generating devices, dongles – physical security devices attached to machines that ensure only the dongle holder can gain access)?

Logical operating system security

- ☑ Do all users on all operating systems have individual IDs?
- ☑ Do all users on all operating systems have passwords?
- ☑ Do you enforce periodic password changes upon all users?
- ☑ Do you have procedures in place for reporting joiner and leaver information to all system administrators?
- ☑ Do all your operating systems log user activity?
- ☑ Do all your operating systems detect and report on irregularities (e.g. failed attempts to access)?
- ☑ Do you periodically review logs of irregularities?

Logical application security

- ☑ Do all users on all applications have individual IDs?
- ☑ Do all users on all applications have passwords?
- ☑ Do you enforce periodic password changes upon all users?
- ☑ Do you have procedures in place for reporting joiner and leaver information to all system administrators?
- ☑ Do all your applications log user activity down to function level (e.g. which user accessed which routines)?
- ☑ Do all your applications have appropriate logical access levels (e.g. read only access, process invoices but not payments etc.).

☑ Do all your applications detect and report on irregularities (e.g. failed attempts to access)?

☑ Do you periodically review logs of irregularities?

☑ Do all your applications produce audit trail time and date stamped down to transaction level (e.g. recording which user made which change on which transaction)?

Logical data security

☑ Do you apply additional logical access controls to drives holding sensitive data?

☑ Have you closed any known 'back doors' into application data?

☑ Is highly sensitive data encrypted whenever stored?

☑ Is sensitive data encrypted whenever it is transmitted (e.g. through a WAN or through the world wide web)?

Holistic information security management and BS7799

This and the preceding chapter should provide most not-for-profit organisations with enough material to manage a secure and safe IT structure. But how do you pull it all together? How can you be assured that everything is under control?

There is an holistic standard for information security management – BS7799 – which can be a useful way of ensuring that you have covered all your security needs and you can use external assessors. BS7799 is not a legal requirement for you, but regulations which *are* binding upon you (e.g. the Data Protection Act, see chapter 11) cite BS7799 as an example of best practice to ensure the security of your data. While smaller not-for-profit organisations probably don't need external certification under BS7799, the principles contained in the standard can be helpful in managing your information security.

BS7799 has two parts:

- Part 1, published in 1995, is a code of practice containing guidance materials to help organisations to implement their own information security systems.
- Part 2, published in 1998, is a specification document against which an organisation can be measured for compliance and certification. It has three sections:
  - section 1 sets out the standard's purpose and definitions
  - section 2 explains the documentation required and risk assessment approach to be used
  - section 3 lists ten topics containing more than 100 controls from which an organisation can make a selection.

TABLE 10.1 Information security management framework

Step number	Step description	Tasks	Outputs
1	Define policy	■ Define and document policy ■ Allocate responsibilities	Information security policy document
2	Scope the information security management system	■ Define the scope in terms of: – organisation – location(s) – assets – technology	Information security management system scoping document
3	Risk assessment	■ Risk assessment for each information system included in scope: – identify assets – identify threats – assess vulnerabilities – assess impacts	Risk management documentation (see checklists in chapter 9 and this chapter)
4	Manage the risk	■ Determine areas and degrees of risk to be managed	Risk management documentation (see checklists in chapter 9 and this chapter)
5	Select controls	■ Select control objectives and controls to be implemented ■ Justify the selection with the results of the risk assessment	Mapping risk management documentation with list of BS7799 control objectives and controls
6	Statement of applicability	■ Prepare a statement of applicability	Document containing list of controls, selections and justifications

One of the key elements of the holistic model is for an organisation to set its own policy and scope of information security management, making your IT security environment 'fit for your purpose'. BS7799 describes this environment as 'the management framework'. Table 10.1, above, summarises the six steps the standard requires for establishing an information security management framework.

Security policy

Your organisation's security policy should cover the following elements:

■ Objective of information security in your organisation.
■ Statements of policy.
■ Outline of responsibilities.
■ Statement of authority and support.

An example policy document is given overleaf.

MODEL 10.1   Information security policy document

Objective

The objective of information security in this organisation is to ensure the confidentiality and integrity of our information and to ensure business continuity by preventing and minimising the impact of adverse security events.

Policy

The organisation aims to protect all its information assets from all threats – internal or external, accidental or deliberate.

This information security policy has been approved by the organisation's chief executive.

The organisation seeks to ensure that it:

- Makes information and information systems appropriately available to users.
- Protects information from unauthorised access.
- Assures confidentiality of information.
- Perpetuates integrity of information.
- Meets its legal and regulatory requirements.
- Has appropriate business continuity plans.
- Investigates any breaches of information security.

- Trains all staff and relevant volunteers to an appropriate level in information security.

The organisation has developed and will maintain appropriate procedures to support this policy.

Responsibilities

The information security manager has direct responsibility for managing this policy and for overseeing its implementation.

All managers are responsible for the implementation of this policy within their area of work and for overseeing adherence by the staff and relevant volunteers in their area of work.

Every member of staff and every relevant volunteer should take personal responsibility for their adherence to this policy.

Signed by the chief executive

_____

Date _____

This policy should be reviewed by the information security manager no later than _____ (*e.g. one year after initial date*)

Information security management system scope

Defining the scope of your information security management system is key. This aspect can be comparatively tricky in not-for-profit organisations, especially when the organisation has general issues regarding the scope of its control. For example, if you are a federated or confederated organisation, you might only have limited ability to control information security in the outlying reaches of your organisation. Indeed, you might need to exclude some aspects of your organisation from the scope of your information security system. Bear in mind, however, that you should be extremely careful about sharing sensitive information assets (e.g. names and addresses of young people in trouble or danger) with parts of your extended organisation that you cannot control and which perhaps do not protect information to your standards.

There are four key aspects to consider and document:

- *Organisation* – as discussed in the above paragraph. Also, you should consider where responsibilities sit within your organisation.
- *Location(s)* – consider which sites are covered and their differing needs. For example, the information security requirements will be significantly greater at headquarters than at a small project with one computer and a modem link to headquarters.
- *Assets* – consider which information assets should be included. An information asset can be any valuable element of your information system, and can include paper documents, software, data files, computers, communications equipment, data media, physical files, safes and intangibles such as intellectual property and human resources.
- *Technology* – consider the various types of technology involved, including computers, communications systems and other relevant equipment.

In a larger organisation, it is usually helpful to use the scoping document (see step 2, table 10.1) as an opportunity to segment the organisation into 'security domains' for management purposes. In any event, you should ensure that the document clarifies security responsibilities throughout the scope.

Control requirements

Part 3 of BS7799 supplies a list of ten topics and subtopics containing more than 100 controls from which an organisation can make a selection. These are:

- information security policy
- security organisation
- assets classification and control
- personnel security
- physical and environmental security
- computer and network management
- system access control
- systems development and maintenance
- business continuity planning
- compliance.

TABLE 10.2 Control requirements

Control topics/subtopics	Objective	Comments and examples
Information security policy		
Policy document	To provide management direction and support for information security	■ See 'Security policy', page 73
Review and evaluation	To ensure that the policy remains appropriate	■ See 'Security policy', page 73
Security organisation		
Information security infrastructure	To manage information security within the organisation	■ See 'Security policy', page 73
Security of third party access	To maintain the security of organisational information processing facilities and information assets accessed by third parties	■ Where third parties have access to some of your information and/or systems, the arrangements should be formalised in contracts between the parties
Outsourcing	To maintain the security of information when the responsibility for information processing has been outsourced to another organisation	■ Your organisation's security requirements should be addressed in the outsourcing contract if you are outsourcing all or part of your IT management
Asset classification and control		
Accountability for assets	To maintain appropriate protection of the organisation's assets	■ Each asset should have a clear, nominated owner ■ You should have an inventory of assets (see chapter 9)
Information classification	To ensure that information assets receive an appropriate level of protection	■ Establish appropriate classification of information ■ Information should be labelled (so you know which part of the classification it falls into)
Personnel security		
Security in job definition and resourcing	To reduce the risks of human error, theft, fraud or misuse of facilities	■ Screening procedures, confidentiality agreements, terms and conditions ■ These aspects should apply to relevant volunteers as well as paid staff
User training	To ensure that users are aware of threats and concerns and are equipped to support the security policy in the course of their work	■ Remember to include relevant volunteers as well as staff
Responding to incidents and malfunctions	To minimise damage from security incidents and malfunctions, to monitor incidents and learn from them	■ Have clear reporting procedures

TABLE 10.2 Control requirements [continued]

Control topics/subtopics	Objective	Comments and examples
Physical and environmental security		
Secure areas	To prevent unauthorised access, damage and interference to premises and information	■ See 'Physical security', in chapter 9
Equipment security	To prevent loss, damage or compromise of assets and interruption to work	■ See 'Physical security', in chapter 9
General controls	To prevent compromise or theft of information and information processing facilities	■ For example, clear desk policy, clear screen policy
Communications and operations management		
Operational procedures and responsibilities	To ensure the correct and secure operation of information processing	■ Clear responsibilities and procedures for the IT operation in your organisation
System planning and acceptance	To minimise the risk of systems failure	■ In particular, pay attention to capacity planning if your organisation is growing fast or has bursts of activity
Protection from malicious software	To safeguard the integrity of software and information	■ Avoiding viruses, worms, Trojan horses, logic bombs etc. (see 'Virus protection', in chapter 7)
Housekeeping	To maintain the integrity and availability of information processing and communication services	■ See 'Backing up', in chapter 9
Network management	To ensure that information in networks is safeguarded and that supporting infrastructure is protected	■ You need to be especially careful if your network interfaces with other organisations'
Media handling and security	To prevent damage to assets and interruptions to activities	■ Refers to data media (disks, tapes etc.)
Exchanges of information and software	To prevent loss, modification or misuse of information exchanged between organisations	■ You should have agreements, procedures and standards in place for sharing information with other organisations ■ This is particularly pertinent for many care organisations who share sensitive information e.g. with statutory authorities
Access control		
Business requirement for system access	To control access to information	■ You should have policies on information dissemination and the authorisation of access to information

TABLE 10.2 Control requirements [continued]

Control topics/subtopics	Objective	Comments and examples
User access management	To prevent unauthorised access to information systems	■ You should have procedures and clear responsibilities for controlling the allocation of access rights
User responsibilities	To prevent unauthorised user access	■ Make sure that users are aware of their responsibilities with regard to access controls
Network access control	Protection of networks	■ Control interfaces between your organisation's networks and other organisations' and/or public networks
Operating system access control	To prevent unauthorised computer access	■ It should be possible to identify and verify the identity of users, record system accesses (including failed attempts), provide authentication controls (e.g. passwords) and restrict connection times where appropriate
Application access control	To prevent unauthorised access to information held in information systems	■ Each system should have access control policies ■ Sensitive systems should be isolated from other systems
Monitoring system access and use	To detect unauthorised activities	■ For example, event logging and usage monitoring
Mobile computing and teleworking	To ensure information security when using mobile computing and teleworking facilities	■ Needs are likely to be location and/or function dependant
Systems development and maintenance		
Security requirements of systems	To ensure security is built into information systems	■ In particular, make sure that you include control requirements in system requirements specifications
Security in application systems	To prevent loss, modification or misuse of user data in application systems	■ Validation of input, control of processing, authentication of messaging and validation of output
Cryptographic controls	To protect the confidentiality, authenticity or integrity of information	■ For example, encryption, digital signatures, cryptographic keys, non-repudiation services
Security of system files	To ensure that IT projects and support activities are conducted in a secure manner	■ Particularly important during system implementations and/or upgrades
Security in development and support processes	To maintain the security of application system software and information	■ Especially needed in organisations which undertake software developments

TABLE 10.2 Control requirements [continued]

Control topics/subtopics	Objective	Comments and examples
Business continuity management		
Aspects of business continuity management	To counteract interruptions to activities and protect critical processes from the impact of major failures or disasters	■ See 'IT business continuity', in chapter 9
Compliance		
Compliance with legal requirements	To avoid breaches of any criminal law, civil law, statutory obligations, regulatory requirements, contractual obligations or security requirements	■ Identify applicable 'rules' ■ Respect intellectual property rights ■ Consider requirements in other countries if your organisation transmits data overseas
Review of security policy and technical compliance	To ensure compliance of systems with organisational security policies and standards	■ Unrecognised failure to comply is a common risk
System audit considerations	To maximise the effectiveness of and minimise interference to or from the system audit process	■ Controls to safeguard the audit process itself ■ Seek to minimise the disruption to the organisation

MODEL 10.2 Extract from a statement of applicability

Control	Selected	Justification
Establish agreements for electronic or manual exchange of information between organisations	Yes	Highlighted in risk assessment as high severity, high likelihood, as our organisation needs to exchange highly sensitive childcare data with statutory authorities. Currently done manually but plans for some electronic links.
Protection for media being transported	Yes	Currently done through secure couriers. Planned electronic links will mostly be logical (e.g. encrypted e-mail) but some might be physical (e.g. encrypted files on disks).
Electronic commerce protection	Yes	Increasing amounts of procurement done electronically.
Policy for use of electronic mail	Yes	See 'Electronic Mail Usage Policy, ref X.
Policies and guidelines for use of electronic office systems	Yes	See our 'Office Users' Guide', ref ZZ.
Formal authentication process before information is made publicly available	No	Organisation is so sensitive we don't make information publicly available.
Procedures and controls for information exchange through voice, facsimile, video communications etc.	Yes	Voice mail and facsimile used heavily, see 'Office Users' Guide', ref ZZ/WW. No imminent plans for video communications.

Table 10.2 (pages 76–9) sets out the topics, objectives and subtopics for controls. Each subtopic includes one or more controls suggested in BS7799.

Statement of applicability

Once you have done your risk assessment and decided how to manage your organisation's risks, you should be able to go through the list of controls in BS7799 part 2 section 3 quickly and decide which are applicable to you, which aren't and why. The output of that exercise is the statement of applicability. An example extract is shown on page 79.

Summary

- Logical security protects your intangible information assets (e.g. your data).
- An holistic information security management system, BS7799, can help you to pull all your information security needs together, even if you choose not to opt for external assessment.
- Key to information security management is your organisation defining its own policies and scope of security need before assessing risks and deciding what controls to put in place.
- Not-for-profit organisations, both large and small, are obliged to address these issues – it should be possible for you to scale what you do about them accordingly.

Data protection

CHAPTER OBJECTIVES

In this chapter we shall:

- Explain your obligations under the Data Protection Act 1998.
- Explode some of the myths about the data protection legislation.
- Provide some practical pointers on how to comply.

Data protection – the basics

The Data Protection Act 1998 is concerned with 'personal data', i.e. information about living, identifiable individuals. This need not be particularly sensitive information and can be as little as a name and address. The Act confers certain rights upon individuals ('data subjects') and certain obligations upon those who record and use personal information ('data controllers'). The legislation exists to protect individuals from the misuse of personal information that organisations hold about them.

The purposes of the legislation are as follows:

- An organisation that wishes to hold personal information should be entered into a data protection register.
- The uses that the organisation intends to make of such information should be defined and declared in advance.
- The information should not be used for illegal or immoral purposes.
- The person whom the information is about should be aware of and should have consented to the purpose to which the information is being put.

- That person should have the right to full access to the information held on them (the organisation is permitted to charge a nominal fee for supplying such information).
- The information should be correct, up to date and should not be excessive.

The eight data protection principles set out in Schedule 1 of the 1998 Act are shown below.

Data protection principles

1 The actual collection of data should be fair and lawful
2 Data should be obtained for specific lawful purposes and should not be processed for other incompatible reasons
3 The data that is collected should be relevant to the purpose for which it is being collected and the quantity collected should be appropriate
4 Personal data should be accurate and up to date
5 Data should not be kept for longer than is necessary for the processing purpose
6 The person whom the information is about has certain basic rights and the information should be processed in accordance with those rights
7 Data should be appropriately secured
8 Data should only be transferred outside the European Economic Area (EEA – EC members states plus Iceland, Liechtenstein and Norway) where similar standards of care apply in those other territories

The Data Protection Act 1998 and key dates for compliance

The data protection principles of the Data Protection Act 1998, although stated for the first time in the new Act, are similar in effect to the preceding legislation (the 1984 Act). The new Act is somewhat more stringent and is harmonising the UK legislation with the EU Data Protection Directive (05/46/EC). The Data Protection Commissioner (previously the Data Protection Registrar) is an independent officer appointed by the Queen who reports directly to Parliament. The key extension to the law is that the new Act applies to manual records 'forming part of a relevant filing system' (i.e. any structured information such as a card index of names and addresses) as well as computerised records. The new Act can be enforced even against organisations which are exempt from notification if they are in breach of the principles, and a person adversely affected by a breach of the Act can claim compensation for damages. There are several other extensions to the legislation.

The new Act came into force from 1 March 2000. However, automated data which is subject to processing already under way (or forming part of an 'accessible file' that existed) before 24 October 1998 will be exempt from most of the additional requirements of the new Act until 23 October 2001. Manual data forming part of a relevant filing system will, subject to certain conditions, be exempt from the new Act until 23 October 2001 and will enjoy limited exemption from some of the principles until 2007. Despite these limited exemptions, it is good practice to start working wholly within the requirements of the new Act as soon as possible. It is hard to imagine a not-for-profit organisation which would fall outside the scope of this legislation.

Conditions under Schedule 2 of the 1998 Act

Schedule 2 of the 1998 Act provides that processing may only be carried out where at least one of the following conditions has been satisfied:

- The individual has consented to the processing.
- The processing is necessary for the performance of a contract with the individual.
- The processing is required under a legal obligation.
- The processing is necessary to protect the vital interests of the individual.
- The processing is needed to carry out public functions.
- The processing is necessary in order to pursue the legitimate interests of the data controller or certain third parties (unless prejudicial to the interests of the individual).

Stricter conditions apply to the processing of sensitive data. This category includes information relating to racial or ethnic origin, political opinions, religious or other beliefs, trades union membership, health, sex life and criminal convictions. Data held by not-for-profit organisations commonly falls within this stricter category. Where such data is being processed, not only must the controller meet the requirements of the principles and Schedule 2, but processing is prohibited unless at least one of the conditions of Schedule 3 can be satisfied (see below).

Stricter conditions under Schedule 3 of the 1998 Act and myths about them

There is a great deal of myth about this category, the most common of which is that you must have explicit consent from the data subject in order to process sensitive data. In fact, there are several acceptable reasons for holding such data (many of which often apply to data held by not-for-profit organisations). For this reason, we have set out a comprehensive list of Schedule 3 conditions below, to enable you to decide whether your organisation's holding of sensitive data is justified.

Schedule 3 of the new Act provides that processing may only be carried out where at least one of the Schedule 2 conditions and at least one of the following conditions has been satisfied:

- The data subject has given their explicit consent to the processing of the personal data.
- The processing is necessary for the purposes of exercising or performing any right or obligation, which is conferred or imposed by law on the data controller in connection with employment.
- The processing is necessary in order to protect the vital interests of the data subject or another person, in a case where:
    - consent cannot be given by or on behalf of the data subject, or
    - the data controller cannot reasonably be expected to obtain the consent of the data subject, or
    - the vital interests of another person need to be protected, in a case where consent by or on behalf of the data subject has been unreasonably withheld.
- The processing:
    - is carried out in the course of its legitimate activities by any body or association which exists for political, philosophical, religious or trades union purposes and which is not established or conducted for profit
    - is carried out with appropriate safeguards for the rights and freedoms of data subjects
    - relates only to individuals who are either members of the body or association or who have regular contact with it in connection with its purposes
    - does not involve disclosure of the personal data to a third party without the consent of the data subject.
- The information contained in the personal data has been made public as a result of steps deliberately taken by the data subject.
- The processing:
    - is necessary for the purpose of, or in connection with, any legal proceedings (including prospective legal proceedings)
    - is necessary for the purpose of obtaining legal advice
    - is otherwise necessary for the purposes of establishing, exercising or defending legal rights.
- The processing is necessary:
    - for the administration of justice, or

- for the exercise of any functions conferred by or under any enactment, or
- for the exercise of any functions of the Crown, a Minister of the Crown or a government department.

■ The processing is necessary for medical purposes (including the purposes of preventative medicine, medical diagnosis, medical research, the provision of care and treatment and the management of health care services) and is undertaken by:
  - a health professional (as defined in the Act), or
  - a person who owes a duty of confidentiality, which is equivalent to that which would arise if that person were a health professional.

■ The processing:
  - is of sensitive personal data consisting of information as to racial or ethnic origin
  - is necessary for the purpose of identifying or keeping under review the existence or absence of equality of opportunity or treatment between persons of different racial or ethnic origins, with a view to enabling such equality to be promoted or maintained
  - is carried out with appropriate safeguards for the rights and freedoms of data subjects.

■ The personal data is processed in circumstances specified in an order made by the Secretary of State.

A helpful guide to compliance

The following checklist and comments should help you to identify the main aspects that require attention and to comply. The nature and extent of actions required are relative and depend on your specific organisation and the purposes for which you are using data. However, if you answer no to any of the questions, you need to do something about it.

DATA PROTECTION CHECKLIST

Question	Yes/no	Notes and comments
Awareness		
Are you aware of the current data protection legislation and its implications for your organisation?		The text contained in this book should be sufficient for most not-for-profit organisations, but if, for example, your work with sensitive data is borderline you might need further detail and guidance on the implications for you.

Question	Yes/no	Notes and comments
Have you formally assigned the responsibilities of data protection officer to an individual in your organisation?		In small not-for-profit organisations, this might often come down to you.
Is your data protection officer aware of the requirements of the current data protection legislation?		
Are you aware of all the purposes for which personal data is being used, and of all the data collection methods used within your organisation?		Not-for-profit organisations often have a myriad of small databases, many of which need to be brought in to the data protection regime. A data protection audit can be a good entrée to eliminating duplication and harmonising your work with personal data.
Have you conducted a data protection audit to ensure that you are aware of all aspects of your work which should be notified to the Data Protection Commissioner?		Bear in mind that spreadsheets and word processing tables with personal data in them fall within the scope of relevant data under the legislation, as do structured manual records.
Have you ensured that all relevant staff are trained and/or made aware of the data protection requirements of their work?		You should also ensure that appropriate volunteers are trained and made aware. You also need mechanisms in place to ensure that new staff are trained and made aware.

Data collection

Question	Yes/no	Notes and comments
Are you informing data subjects of the purposes for which the required data is held, the identity of your data controller and any data transfer to a third party?		Not-for-profit organisations that have, for example, bought and/or sold donor or membership lists should think carefully about meeting the legal requirements in this area.
Are you obtaining all your personal data in a lawful manner?		
Are you sure that the personal data your organisation collects is adequate, relevant and not excessive?		Just because it is appropriate for you to hold an item of data for some individuals does not mean that it appropriate for you to keep that data item for *all* individuals – this is especially relevant for not-for-profit organisations involved in diverse activities.
Are your data collection people reliable in their collection of data – i.e. honest, discreet, professional and security conscious?		
Do you have security measures in place to enable you to monitor the activities of your data collection people?		
Where data collection is undertaken on your behalf by a third party, do you have signed agreements in place requiring that		Many not-for-profit organisations use third parties for this purpose – you should ensure that you are nevertheless fulfilling

Question	Yes/no	Notes and comments
third party to comply with your data protection measures?		your data protection responsibilities, albeit through an third party.
Do people handling personal data sign confidentiality agreements or equivalent?		

Data processing and storage

Question	Yes/no	Notes and comments
Where data processing and/or storage is undertaken on your behalf by a third party, do you have signed agreements in place requiring that third party to comply with your data protection measures?		Many not-for-profit organisations use third parties for this purpose – you should ensure that you are nevertheless fulfilling your data protection responsibilities, albeit through an third party.
Are you sure your data is used only for the purposes covered by your data protection notification and those purposes specified to each data subject?		
If you use an automated system for decision making (e.g. skills scoring for potential recruits), would you be able to explain the logic of this system to data subjects?		Rarely used by not-for-profit organisations at present, but this is a defined right for data subjects.
If a data subject insists on not being part of an automated process, do you have alternative non-automated processes available?		
Do you have a process in place which enables you to provide a data subject with the personal data you hold about them?		
Do you have a process in place which enables you to prevent processing likely to cause a data subject damage or distress?		
Do you have processes in place which enable you to prevent a data subject's information being used for direct marketing?		
Do you make reasonable efforts to ensure the accuracy of the information on your system?		
Do you have a process in place to correct erroneous data?		
Do you inform relevant third parties when incorrect data is corrected?		
Do you only hold data for as long as it is required?		Regardless of the legislation, not-for-profit organisations should have such policies in place for good practice, especially where the data is sensitive.

Question	Yes/no	Notes and comments
Do you have policies for archiving and cleaning up your data to ensure that only current data is maintained?		
Do you have adequate security to ensure that it is not possible for unauthorised people to gain access to your data?		The level of security should be appropriate for the nature of personal data held. Although the Data Protection Act does not mandate security standards, it suggests that BS 7799, the Information Security Management standard, is an acceptable standard (see chapter 10 – 'Information security').

Data transfers

Do you conduct all your data transactions within the European Economic Area (EEA)?		
If you obtain, process or transfer data outside the EEA, do you know what form of data protection and information security is used in those countries?		This requirement is relevant for some charities, e.g. those who are active in developing countries.

Notification

Have you notified the Data Protection Commissioner of personal data held and its purposes?		Formerly known as Data Protection Registrar.
Was your last notification done within the past three years?		
Have your systems, processes and data requirements remained unchanged since your last notification?		
Have you notified the Data Protection Commissioner about any changes in notified information?		
Do you have procedures in place for dealing with any formal complaints lodged with the Commissioner?		
Do your systems development and maintenance procedures include the requirements of the notification process?		

Summary

- Data protection requirements under the 1998 Act are more onerous than under the previous legislation.
- Almost all not-for-profit organisations have obligations under this legislation, so if you haven't yet made sure that you comply with the new rules, it's time to get on with it.

- The obligations and conditions are mostly sensible, despite the many myths one hears to the contrary.
- The details and checklists in this book should be sufficient to help most not-for-profit organisations to comply, but if your circumstances are complex or sensitive you would do well to seek expert guidance where in doubt.

Health and safety

CHAPTER OBJECTIVES

In this chapter we shall:

- Explain the scope and purpose of the relevant health and safety regulations and how the defined terms in the regulations should be interpreted for not-for-profit organisations.
- Set out a checklist with tips on how not-for-profit organisations can set about complying.

Regulations – scope and purpose

The relevant Health and Safety legislation in this area is the **Health and Safety (Display Screen Equipment) Regulations 1992**. This legislation is based on an EC Directive, issued in 1990, to cover the health and safety aspects of working with visual display units (VDUs), also referred to as DSE (display screen equipment). In January 1993 this Directive became part of UK legislation under the Health and Safety at Work Act. The regulations cover not only the equipment, but also the software and environment. They use the term 'workstation' to cover all of these aspects, including furniture, lighting, temperature, humidity etc.

The regulations require 'users' and 'operators' to be identified and a suitable and sufficient assessment to be made of all workstations with a view to reducing risks. A 'user' is defined as an employee who habitually uses display screen equipment as a significant part of their normal work. An 'operator' is defined as a self-employed person working within an organisation.

Not-for-profit organisations should interpret the regulations as applying to all employees, temporary staff, volunteers and beneficiaries who habitually use display screen equipment. It is the organisation's responsibility to comply with the regulations and also the responsibility of individuals themselves to ensure that the facilities and equipment are used correctly.

The aim of the regulations is to prevent health problems by encouraging good ergonomic design of equipment, furniture, the working environment and the job. The Health and Safety Executive believes the cost of complying with the regulations may be offset by reductions in sickness absence or gains in productivity. The regulations place an obligation on employers to:

- Analyse workstations and reduce health and safety risks.
- Ensure workstations meet minimum ergonomic requirements.
- Provide information about risks and measures.
- Plan daily work routine for users.
- Offer eye tests and special glasses if necessary.
- Provide health and safety training.

Regulations – checklist and tips

The following checklist and comments should help you to identify aspects that require attention and help you to comply. Ergonomic recommendations are relative and depend on the individual, the task and the equipment being used. The notes and comments with the checklist are designed to help not-for-profit organisations to comply without bursting the budget. Remember, if you answer no to any of the questions, you need to do something about it.

HEALTH AND SAFETY CHECKLIST

Question	Yes/no	Notes and comments (some from a not-for-profit organisation's perspective)
Workstation environment		
Is there adequate ventilation?		Lack of ventilation can cause discomfort, sore eyes and skin rashes. In particular, laser printers and photocopiers should be sited in well ventilated areas.
Is the humidity adequate?		Electrical equipment produces dry heat – consider placing a broad-leaved plant or a bowl of water with a wick in the work area to increase humidity and reduce static electricity. Ensure that water is kept away from electrical equipment.

Question	Yes/no	Notes and comments (some from a not-for-profit organisation's perspective)
Are noise levels acceptable e.g. from a printer or PC?		The British Standards Institution suggests a maximum of 55 decibels for work requiring sustained concentration and 60 decibels for other workstation work. Noisy impact printers should ideally have acoustic hoods to reduce noise.
Is cabling secure and tidy?		Uncontrolled wires and cables are a common cause of accidents. Ideally they should be confined in desk brackets or trunking.
Is there sufficient working space?		For example, can users and operators change position and vary movements? Don't forget that you need to take individuals' special needs into account, especially if you are offering a service to beneficiaries with special needs.
Visual display units (VDUs)		
Are you able to swivel and tilt your screen?		The angle of vision normally recommended is 30 to 45 degrees below the normal horizontal.
Is your screen free from glare and reflections?		Where possible, the VDU should be at right angles to the window. Where glare cannot be avoided, you should fit anti-glare screens to the VDUs. Shop carefully for anti-glare screens, as some suppliers make extravagant claims about expensive screens. Try before you buy if possible.
Can you easily alter the brightness and contrast?		The brightness of the VDU should be adjusted to suit the lighting conditions in the room. Where natural light is available, this often requires the ability to change brightness and/or contrast during the day as the ambient light changes.
Is the screen image flicker free?		Defective VDUs should be replaced. In general, working with VDUs does not cause epilepsy, but in the rare case of photo-sensitive epilepsy, VDU screen flicker might affect people adversely.
Do you regularly clean the screen?		Screens should be kept free of dust and finger marks. Special anti-static cleaners are advisable, but regular wiping with a soft cloth or tissue is usually sufficient.
Keyboard		
Is your keyboard independent of the main unit?		Modern keyboards on desktop computers have 'advisable' (i.e. detachable, tiltable) keyboards.

Question	Yes/no	Notes and comments (some from a not-for-profit organisation's perspective)
Can the surface angle of the keyboard be adjusted?		Laptop computers usually do not have them, which is one of several reasons why prolonged use of laptop computers is not recommended.
Is there adequate space in front of the keyboard to rest your wrists?		Approximately 100mm (4") is recommended. If the keyboard is high, you might use some padding in front of the keyboard to support the wrists.
Are the keys easily readable?		The symbols on the keys should be legible and not cause reflections.
Can the keys be depressed without excessive effort?		If you are using an older computer with an inappropriate keyboard, consider replacing the keyboard even if you cannot afford to replace the computer.

Chairs

Question	Yes/no	Notes and comments
Does your chair have a five point base?		Essentially, chairs should:
Is your chair stable and safe from tipping over?		■ support the back in its natural curve ■ distribute the body's weight evenly ■ minimise pressure on the thighs behind the knees.
Is the seating height easily adjustable?		
Is the height of the backrest adjustable?		Ideally, individuals should try several different styles of chair before buying a new one to ensure that the individual is comfortable.
Can the backrest be adjusted forwards and backwards?		
Can adjustments be made easily and safely from the seated position?		Again, you should consider individuals with special needs on a case by case basis.
Are the castors free and working?		
Is the floor surface sound and stable?		The floor should allow the wheels of chairs to run freely and should not produce excessive static electricity.

Footrests

Question	Yes/no	Notes and comments
When seated comfortably do your feet rest firmly on the floor?		You should provide footrests for anyone who requires one – usually relevant for people under 1600 mm (5ft 3") or those with relatively short legs. Footrests ensure that feet and legs are comfortably supported and that blood supply at the back of the knees is not restricted.
If no, are footrests provided?		
If footrests are used are they easily adjustable: ■ in height ■ in inclination?		

Question	Yes/no	Notes and comments (some from a not-for-profit organisation's perspective)
Desks		
Is the desk surface sufficient to allow a flexible arrangement of papers and other equipment?		The British Standards Institution recommends a minimum of 1200×600 mm ($48'' \times 24''$) and an optimum size of 1600×800 mm ($63'' \times 32''$). In any event, the desk should be deep enough from front to back to allow room for the system unit, keyboard and other related equipment and still leave at least 100 mm ($4''$) at the front of the desk to allow space to rest your wrists when not typing.
Is the desk surface non-reflective?		
Is the leg room sufficient to allow unobstructed turning?		
Do you use a document holder for copy typing?		
Is it positioned next to and in the same plane as the screen?		The desk should be of reasonable height to allow sufficient clearance for legs. Suggested desk height is 720 mm ($29''$) for fixed height desks and 680 to 760 mm ($27''$ to $30''$) for adjustable desks. The desk should not be so high that the chair cannot be adjusted to fit it or the feet cannot rest comfortably on the floor or footrest.
Is adequate storage space provided for copies, handbooks, documents, personal belongings etc.?		
Lighting		
Where natural light exists, have steps been taken to reduce glare/reflections, e.g. positioning of the equipment, fitted blinds?		General lighting should illuminate the entire room to an adequate standard. Desk lamps may be required to provide an appropriate contrast between the screen and the background environment, taking into account the type of work and an individual's needs.
Is the artificial light sufficient but not too bright?		
Are desk lamps provided where necessary?		Be careful when positioning desk lamps to ensure that they do not adversely affect nearby workstations.
General		
Do you take a break from your workstation every hour?		Potential problems arising from not taking regular breaks include back ache, circulatory problems, eye strain and repetitive strain injury (RSI).
		RSI can be caused by repetitive movements, awkward working positions, inadequate rest breaks and poor office and equipment design. Examples of RSI are tenosynovitis (inflammation of the tendon sheaths in hands, wrists and arms), writers' cramp and tennis elbow. The normal symptoms are pain or discomfort in the upper limbs. If discomfort persists even when taking proper breaks and sitting properly, the affected person should stop

Question	Yes/no	Notes and comments (some from a not-for-profit organisation's perspective)
		using display screen equipment and consult a doctor promptly. This problem seems particularly common in not-for-profit organisations, possibly as a result of the enthusiasm of some volunteers and staff and high transaction volumes in several aspects of not-for-profit organisations' work.
Do you offer eye tests to 'users'?		You are obliged to offer eye tests to users and offer special glasses if necessary. There is no evidence to suggest that VDU work causes eye problems of itself, but it can make people more aware of existing untreated eye conditions. Eye strain can be caused by: ■ close focusing for too long without sensible breaks ■ insistent glare ■ reflection from windows and other light sources ■ a flickering image on the screen ■ low humidity levels, especially in the case of contact lens wearers. Most people normally read with a document 330 to 360 mm (13" to 14") away from their eyes, whereas the normal distance for reading from a VDU is about 530 mm (21"). People who normally wear glasses for reading sometimes find it helpful to have a special pair of glasses for working with VDUs.
Has your PC been checked for safety under the Electricity at Work Regulations?		Health and Safety Executive guidance states that computer equipment should be examined annually for electrical and associated faults. In addition, the equipment should be safety tested every five years. You might wish to check that your maintenance contract covers these issues.

Summary

■ Health and safety regulations are designed to help you to be healthier, safer and more efficient in the long run – ultimately they are therefore a good thing.

■ Not-for-profit organisations should include part-time employees, volunteers and beneficiaries who use computer equipment within their definition of users for the purpose of complying with this legislation.

- If you apply common sense to complying, ensuring compliance should help your not-for-profit organisation become more economic and efficient.

Part 3

IT systems

IT systems – using this part

Most of this part should be useful for all not-for-profit organisations, whatever their size. Chapter 13 in particular applies to all elements of the sector – from tiny to large. Regardless of size, if you are selecting standard packages and/or systems suppliers beyond the standard office tool kits described in that chapter, you should benefit from reading all the chapters in this part.

If you are interested in small not-for-profit organisations, which are likely to meet their needs with standard office tool kits alone, you should still skim chapter 14 for ideas and read chapter 15 to help ensure that your project, however small, delivers the results you want.

Standard tools and packages and bespoke solutions

CHAPTER OBJECTIVES

In this chapter we shall:

- Explain the main components of office tool kits and discuss the (rather limited) choices available.
- Define standard packages and bespoke solutions.
- Outline the arguments and factors you should consider when choosing which route to go.
- Set out some examples of tools for each main type of application used by not-for-profit organisations of various sizes.

What do we mean by 'office tool kits'?

Figure 13.1 (overleaf) illustrates a fairly standard example of an IT user's desktop in a not-for-profit (or for that matter, just about any) organisation.

In part 2 we discussed the main issues relating to machines and operating systems (computer programs that enable users' programs to interact with the machines). Most users today will have some form of personal computer on their desktop. The vast majority of those computers will grant access to a collection of office software. We refer to this collection of office software as the 'office tool kit'. Although it is possible to buy these tools individually, most users take advantage of bundled pricing and purchase a collection of office software as a suite, such as Microsoft Office or Lotus SmartSuite.

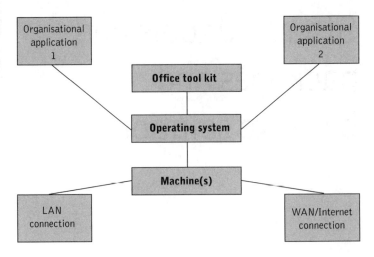

FIGURE 13.1 Typical IT user's desktop

What do you get in an office tool kit?

The table opposite sets out the main office software one might find in a not-for-profit organisation worker's office tool kit. Not all kits include all these tools, but many not-for-profits do not need all of them.

Pick a brand

Although there are several tool kits on the market, at the time of writing the vastly predominant one is Microsoft Office. The Office suite comes in various editions (standard, small business edition, premium, professional). The main alternative suppliers are Corel WordPerfect Suite and Lotus SmartSuite, but their market share has been steadily falling for the past few years, which has been making the market less competitive. Smaller charities might consider scaled down tools such as Microsoft Works as a cheap, cheerful and quick to learn tool kit in circumstances where only basic requirements are envisaged. Another alternative, Sun's Star Office tool kit, is downloadable from the world wide web. At time of writing, the basic Star Office suite is free.

Weighing up the tool kit options

Although smaller/cheaper options might seem attractive at first, not-for-profit organisations should always consider the hidden

TABLE 13.1 Tools you are likely to see

Tool	Description	Charity usage	Product examples
Word processing	Primarily for the sophisticated manipulation of text	Most charity workers who use personal computers use regularly (i.e. most days)	*Microsoft Word, Lotus Word Pro, Corel WordPerfect*
Spreadsheet	Primarily for the sophisticated manipulation of numbers	Some charity workers use regularly, many use occasionally	*Microsoft Excel, Lotus 1-2-3, Corel Quattro Pro*
Presentation graphics	Primarily for presenting words, numbers, charts and pictures	Some charity workers use regularly, some use occasionally	*Microsoft Powerpoint, Lotus Freelance*
Desk top publishing	For producing publishing quality publications	Some charity workers use regularly	*Quark XPress, Pagemaker, Page Plus*
Electronic mail	For communicating internally and/or with the outside world	Many charity workers use regularly, some charities restrict the ad hoc use of e-mail	*Microsoft Outlook, Lotus cc: mail, GroupWise*
Personal organisation	For managing calendars, tasks, contacts, work schedules etc.	Some charity workers use regularly	*Microsoft Outlook, Lotus Organiser, GroupWise*
Database	For building the sophisticated storage, linkage and retrieval of information	Some charity workers use regularly, many charities restrict the ad hoc use of databases	*Microsoft Access, Lotus Approach, Corel Paradox*

costs of training and compatibility before making choices based on price alone. For example, staff effectiveness can be seriously impaired if you are using non-standard tool kits. Weighing up these issues has in recent years tended to drive most organisations towards choosing Microsoft Office.

Although suppliers' policies towards voluntary sector discounts vary from time to time, it is currently possible to get significant voluntary sector discount on most suites. Suppliers of computers frequently bundle an office suite as part of a deal when selling machines. It is always worth checking whether such bundled software meets your requirements, as the benefits of such a deal can soon evaporate if you need to buy even one individual component at full price to supplement a bundled suite. Organisations also need to consider whether such a deal is really a bargain, especially if they are eligible for significant voluntary sector discounts.

Although it is usually technically possible to exchange information between different office tool kits, it makes a great deal of sense for an organisation to standardise on a single collection of tools. Some people will make a big fuss if you try to wrench them away from their pet office tool kit, but it really is worth putting up with the noise in the short term to achieve standardisation. Standardisation helps enormously with ongoing support, enabling users to help each other and thus minimise the overall cost. Standardisation also helps to facilitate information exchange between users; such exchange is often key to the benefits your organisation can get from IT.

Standard packages and bespoke solutions

Office tool kits, discussed above, can be viewed as a particular sub-category of standard packages as defined below. Almost all computer users use office tool kits to some extent. Smaller organisations can sometimes choose to use elements of office tool kits as an alternative to the more sophisticated standard packages (see 'Deciding between tool kits, standard packages and bespoke solutions', below). Think of office tool kits as being analogous with an 'off the peg' uniform.

Standard packages are software products produced to meet specific functions, such as accounting, fundraising, payroll, etc. Packages are normally sold in a standard form, i.e. everyone who buys a standard software package is buying the same computer code. Packages are often configurable, i.e. you set up the software to operate the way you want it to operate, but nevertheless the software is the same as that being used by others. This is not the same thing as customising a standard package (see definition of bespoke solutions, below). Think of standard packages as being analogous with 'off the peg' garments in a department store, sold for special events.

Bespoke software solutions are software products written specifically for you to your specification. Think of bespoke solutions as being analogous with a made-to-measure garment manufactured for you by a tailor. Bespoke solutions are not normally advisable for not-for-profit organisations.

Deciding between tool kits, standard packages and bespoke solutions

Office tool kits have been sold with more and more features 'thrown in' to each release, as suppliers compete for market share. Now that Microsoft dominates the market, the main competition is apathy (reluctance to spend time and money on upgrading), so suppliers try to entice people to upgrade to get more features. For smaller organisations, this standard tool kit provides enough features to prevent them from needing many other packages. For example, Microsoft Outlook's contact management features (such as the address book) will be sufficient for some small not-for-profit organisations, so they would not need a more sophisticated contact management or fundraising system. It very much depends on what your organisation needs to do.

Generally, the cheapest and fastest way to implement new systems is to use standard application packages. Such packages should preferably be well proven (i.e. with lots of existing, happy users) and should be possible to implement with the minimum disruption. Selection of such packages, however, will normally require compromises to be taken over functionality. If no package comes close enough to meeting your requirements, it may be necessary to have a 'bespoke' system developed for you. Not-for-profit organisations, like most organisations, usually begin the selection process from the premise that they want their solution to be based on standard packages. Once they have gauged diverse opinions and specified their requirements, it sometimes becomes clear that no standard packages come close to meeting all the requirements. Resolving this paradox requires sound judgement in scaling down expectations and specifying requirements again in line with pragmatic IT opportunities.

Bespoke developments may be done using internal staff resources, contract staff or a software house. They tend to be expensive and take a considerable time to reach full implementation. An even greater cost lies in maintaining and enhancing a bespoke development. Organisations should only go along this route if it means significant comparative advantage and the only available package solutions would mean making unacceptable compromises. The need for bespoke systems in not-for-profit organisations is very rare – they are almost always limited to specialised areas of need where the only available packages are overly complex for the not-for-profit organisation concerned.

Indeed, complexity is an important factor to take into account when choosing between standard packages and bespoke solutions. An organisation that processes large volumes of data in an uncomplicated way is almost certainly going to be better off with a standard package, even if it needs to compromise on some desirable features to achieve that standardisation.

There are compromises available when an organisation has one or two unique needs in an otherwise standard requirement, such as:

- Customising an element of a standard package.
- Writing a small 'bolt-on' bespoke application to work beside or with a standard package.

Although the above approaches reduce the risks in bespoke development, not-for-profit organisations should think long and hard before following the bespoke line. Just because 'what you do' is complex does not necessarily mean that there is benefit in automating all of it. Indeed, for many complex elements of work, relatively simple automation is often preferable. Legacies administration is a good example. Good legacy administrators can describe a myriad of complicated procedures and processes they follow and decisions they make on a regular basis. A straightforward legacies administration system can support those activities well with appropriate record keeping, diarising, correspondence standardisation and financial monitoring. A system seeking to automate all procedures, processes and decisions quickly becomes overly complex and unwieldy.

Because software suppliers know that authors like us try to put readers like you off bespoke solutions, some will try to tout their database and workflow bespoking tools as 'highly config-

TABLE 13.2 Possible solutions

Function	Large charity	Medium-sized charity	Small charity
Size indicators:			
Annual income	£5 million or more	£500,000 to £5 million	Less than £500,000
Staff	200 or more	20 to 200	Fewer than 20
Accounting and payroll			
Size indicators:			
Transactions per year	10,000 or more	500 to 10,000	Fewer than 500
Modules	Ledgers, budgets, job costing, allocations …	Ledgers and budgets	What's a ledger?
Types of tools and packages to consider	Enterprise resource planning systems, mid-range financial systems	Mid-range financial systems, powerful lower-end financial systems	Lower-end financial systems, spreadsheets, manual records
Examples of accounting tools and packages	*Oracle, Peoplesoft, JD Edwards, Lawson, Masterpiece*		*Sage Instant, MYOB, Microsoft Money, TAS Books, Quicken*
	SunAccount, Dynamics, Access Accounting, Scala, Navision, Tetra		
		QuickBooks, Sage Sterling, TAS Business Controller, AccPac, Pegasus Opera	
Examples of payroll solutions	*ADP, CMG, CentreFile, APS,* accountant's bureau service		
		Payroll modules of above accounting packages	
Other things to consider	■ Bureau, shared service solution or business process outsourcing for accounting and/or payroll ■ Auditors'/accountants' requirements ■ References from organisations of similar size and complexity		

urable packages'. Beware! If you are having to write most of the workflow rules for your system and especially if you are having to define the underlying database, you have a bespoke development on your hands with most if not all of the resulting costs, effort and risks.

Guiding examples and thoughts

With the usual caveats about rules of thumb, size measures not applying in all cases and making sure your own organisation's requirements are met, table 13.2 sets out some examples and thoughts on probable, sensible solutions for different sizes of organisations. Remember that you should always follow the process set out in chapter 14 when selecting systems.

TABLE 13.2 Possible solutions [continued]

Function	Large charity	Medium-sized charity	Small charity
Contact management, membership, fundraising			
Size indicators:			
Number of contacts	5,000 or more	300 to 5,000	Fewer than 300
Complexity	Large number of detailed records required on covenants, legacies, membership, sponsorships, donor history ...	Some detail required in some of the areas listed for larger charities	Detailed aspects tend to be low volume and are reasonably easy to record and manage without complex systems
Types of tools and packages to consider	Enterprise fundraising/ membership system, higher end contact management system	Lower end fundraising/ membership system, contact management system	Lower-end contact management system, organisers, card index
Examples of contact management, membership and fundraising systems	Consider more than one of the solutions below, consider modifications and/or bespoke modules *Raiser's Edge, Visual Alms, Care Contacts, Minerva, Genesis, Maximiser Enterprise, Goldmine*		*Microsoft Outlook, GroupWise*
		ACT, Maximiser, Goldmine, Lotus Domino, small bespoke database (e.g. *In Access, Approach or Paradox*)	
Other things to consider	■ Bureau service or business process outsourcing from third party supplier ■ References from other organisations of similar size and complexity		

Summary

- An office tool kit is a collection of basic office software that most people have on their machines (e.g. word processing, spreadsheet, presentation graphics).
- Consider hidden costs (training, compatibility with other organisations) before making a decision solely on price (or lack of price!).
- Whatever you choose, it really is worth standardising within your organisation to minimise support costs and maximise the ease of information exchange.
- Standard packages are usually the quickest and easiest way for not-for-profit organisations to meet their requirements.
- Occasionally not-for-profit organisations will have an unusual requirement which requires bespoke or non-standard software. This route should not be chosen lightly, as the costs, effort and risks involved are comparatively high.

The choosing process and closing the deal

CHAPTER OBJECTIVES

In this chapter we shall:

- Strongly encourage you to follow a proper process for selecting computer applications, even if you are a small organisation with a limited budget .
- Set out the process in sensible stages, with pointers and tips.
- Provide some tips on whether and how to use outside help.
- Set out the tasks required to complete the due diligence process on your decision.
- Provide pointers on agreeing fair and reasonable contracts.

One reason why so many IT projects go wrong

Regardless of size, not-for-profit organisations should follow a proper process for selecting computer software applications. Even if the cost of the software seems relatively low, the 'all-in cost' of a solution, including training and the implementation effort, is usually significant. The cost of failure is usually even higher, when you count the psychological cost and benefits not achieved. Based on empirical evidence, IT systems projects appears to be an inherently risky area of activity. A 1996 study by the University of Sheffield Institute of Work Psychology (Clegg *et al.*, 1996) indicated that more than 80 per cent of IT systems projects were late to a material extent. And according to the 1995 Standish Group CHAOS report (see English, 1995), over 31 per cent of IT systems projects were cancelled before they were completed and 53 per cent of projects cost at least 189 per cent of their original budgets. Only 9 per cent came in on time and on budget. A more recent study by Andrew Taylor (2001) provides little comfort, boasting only 12.7 per cent of projects 'successful', using Standish criteria for success.

People in not-for-profit organisations often express surprise at the above statistics. 'It's not just us charities who botch up IT projects,' they say, 'it's a general syndrome'. Yes it is, but that should not provide comfort. Quite the opposite. If commercial organisations expect to overspend and run late, at least they probably have the excess resources to pay for it. Hopefully the reader is now convinced that there is need for improvement. Using a proper process for choosing the right software is not the only requirement for a successful IT project (other factors are covered throughout this book, not least chapters 3 and 16). Nevertheless, we believe that using a form of the following process minimises the risks and maximises the potential rewards from an IT project. Naturally, the process for smaller solutions is likely to be quicker and less detailed than that for larger solutions. The process and tips set out below can be scaled to suit the size and complexity of your organisation and its needs.

The main stages

The main stages of the process to choose computer software applications should be:

■ Feasibility.
■ Specification of functional requirements.
■ Invitation to tender.
■ Selection of preferred supplier(s).
■ Due diligence contract negotiation and agreement.

The following sections cover each of these in turn. The figure opposite illustrates the decision making processes you should be following as you move through the stages.

Feasibility

This stage is sometimes referred to as the 'business case stage'. The purposes are:

■ Clearly stating objectives and project scope.
■ Defining benefits.
■ Estimating costs, value and risks.

It is astonishing how many IT systems projects are attempted without any feasibility stage at all – this is akin to setting off on a journey without knowing where you are going or why you are going there. Even for smaller projects, we suggest that as a mini-

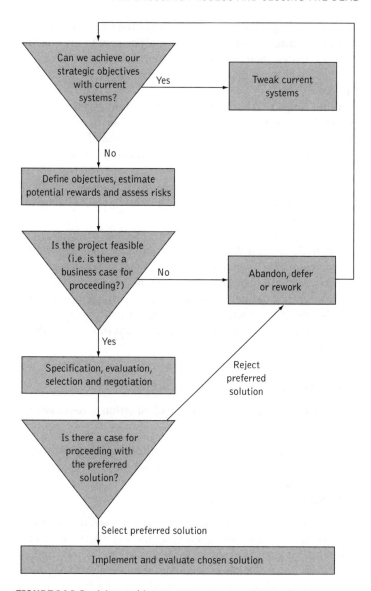

FIGURE 14.1 Decision making process

mum you should define the objectives and attempt to quantify the benefits or rewards sought. It is important at this stage to ensure that appropriate people are consulted, that the project is properly defined and that people understand what is and is not to be included within the scope of the project (see also chapter 16).

To start with, ask the simple question 'can we achieve our strategic objectives with our current systems?' (You might still choose to change systems to improve economy and efficiency, or you might tweak your existing system to achieve the objectives.)

Outline the project objectives in terms of the strategic objectives you are setting out to meet. Your analysis should also include your estimated quantification of potential rewards, estimated costs and a risk-based assessment for each objective and for the project overall.

Don't forget to take risk factors into account, e.g. have you discounted the cash flows of this project with an appropriate risk-adjusted discount factor – i.e. a discount rate that takes into account the amount of risk inherent in the proposed project? How sure are you about your cost estimates and how sure are you that you will achieve the efficiency gains? What is the likelihood of the project failing completely and how much might it have cost you by the time you bail out?

Many projects that easily appear feasible using a simple cost/benefit analysis do not make it past the feasibility hurdle once a reasonable analysis of risk is included. Many systems projects proceed with little or no definition of project objectives and without clearly defined benefits. Lack of definition makes the specification and selection phases quite difficult, to say the least. It really is worth putting some time and effort into the feasibility stage. Template 14.1 might help.

Specification of functional requirements

The purposes of the specification of functional requirements stage are:

- Defining requirements sufficiently to enable users to agree the specification and enable potential suppliers to quote for the software.
- Separating needs from wants.

The specification process should define the scope of the project in more detail and set out the user requirements in the areas to be covered. This stage is essential in beginning to involve users, to help them to understand their requirements and to begin the process of changing working practices. The specification document should form the basis of the invitation to tender and eventually form part of the contract with the selected supplier(s). Ideally, staff engaged on specification work should have both business analysis and IT skills.

There was a time when the specification stage was governed by 'Thumper's Law' $E = mc^2$, where 'm' is the *mass* of the specification document (kilograms weight or centimetres thickness), 'c' is the *clunk* the document makes when it lands on the desk (decibels) and E is the *enormous fee* extracted by professional advisors (£ tens of thousands). In more modern approaches, Thumper's Law no longer applies – the specification document itself should be the

TEMPLATE 14.1 Feasibility

Part 1 – Business case: scope and objectives

```

```

Benefit assessment

```

```

Desired timescale and reasons

```

```

Other relevant points

```

```

Part 2 – Proposed solution: overview

```

```

Suitability of existing systems (with enhancements?)

```

```

Is there commercial software available?

```

```

What are the (rough) estimated costs?

```

```

Is there a low cost option that might achieve most but not all the benefits sought?

```

```

What are the essential service level requirements?

```

```

What are the main risks and how can these be reduced?

```

```

Is use of IT infrastructure required?

```

```

minimum required to explain the system needs for users and to potential suppliers. As a minimum, set out core functions, features, workflows and information needs. If you overspecify, you'll frequently find that you have defined a requirement that only a bespoke development can solve.

The specification document should focus on the trickier and unusual elements of your requirements, where you will need to specify details in order to communicate your needs and clearly

TABLE 14.1 Specification of functional requirements outline

Section title	Section contents	Comments
Executive summary	Précis of document, summarising core functions, features, workflows and information needs	■ If required – smaller organisations might not need ■ Avoid using an executive summary when you want executives to review the whole document
Scope and objectives	The scope of the system sought and the objectives for seeking the system	■ Should normally come from feasibility documentation – see template 14.1
Current situation and future needs	Outline of existing systems, current staffing around those systems, current technical environment (hardware, operating systems, database systems) and estimated volumes, outline of anticipated needs changes, future technical environment and estimated volumes, reasons for seeking systems change	■ Much of this information should come from the feasibility documentation – see template 14.1
Main processes	Workflow diagram(s), explanations of workflow diagram(s)	■ See figure 14.2
Outline user requirements	User needs and wants based on the processes set out in the workflow diagram(s) – make sure that reporting requirements and links with other systems are spelled out here	■ Indicate which requirements are 'needs' (i.e. mandatory) and which are 'wants' (i.e. desirable)
Technical requirements	Include needs and wants relating to user interface (the look and feel of the system), documentation, facilities (e.g. response times, integration mechanisms, links to other software), security, continuity features, support and maintenance	■ Indicate which requirements are 'needs' (i.e. mandatory) and which are 'wants' (i.e. desirable
Data entities and fields	A diagram of the main data entities and a summary of the information you wish to hold for each	■ See figure 14.3 ■ For larger and/or non-standard systems (basic financial software specifications should not need this level of detail)
Classification codes	Set out tables of classification codes	■ For larger and/or non-standard systems (basic financial software specifications should not need this level of detail) ■ Avoid setting out this information if you expect to change these classification codes significantly as part of your system change
Example sets	Forms, reports and listings from the current system	■ Need only apply to non-standard matters ■ Avoid setting out elements that you expect to change substantially and therefore might prove misleading in their current form

indicate where items are essential, highly desirable or simply 'nice to have'. Table 14.1, opposite, provides an outline of a basic specification of functional requirements. Figures 14.2 and 14.3 give examples of workflows.

Invitation to tender

Preparing the invitation to tender entails finding a 'long list' of potentially suitable suppliers and 'topping and tailing' the specification of requirements to describe the tendering and selection process.

Supplement your specification document (see table 14.1) by setting out the selection process, including the envisaged selection and implementation timescales. Ask questions about the suppliers at this stage (e.g. their financial position, the prevalence of the solution(s) they propose or references). Make sure you include tendering contractual matters, such as fees (the usual practice is for you to pay no fee during the tendering process and this should be clearly stated in your invitation to tender document) and state matters of principle for the eventual

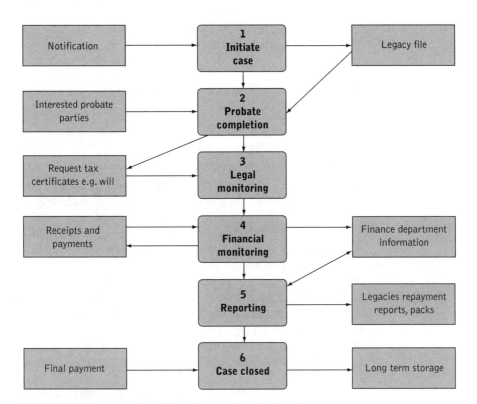

FIGURE 14.2 Example of workflow diagram based on legacies administration

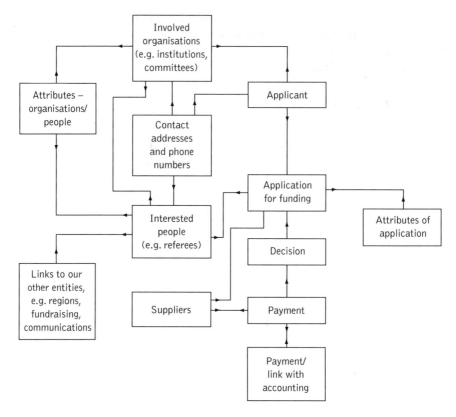

FIGURE 14.3 Example data entity diagram (based on a grant making system)

contracts. The invitation to tender document should include the following:

■ *Introduction* – explain what the invitation to tender is, your confidentiality rules, procedures for tendering (including the fact that you do not intend to pay for proposals) and your selection criteria, including attitude to costs (e.g. the extent to which price is a major factor in your choice). This should be two to three pages.

■ *Background* – give brief information on your organisation, a summary of your requirements, the main reasons and objectives of tendering and the timetable. This should also be two to three pages.

■ *Specification of requirements* – see table 14.1. Exclude your internal management summary and any other confidential information, such as staff names and salaries.

■ *Supplier questionnaire* – ask for company details, company performance, approach to quality, approach to equal opportunities and other ethical issues, staff experience, company experience with similar organisations and similar projects, user base for similar requirements, whether they have a user group, user references, summary of costs and benefits, reservations about the proposal, modifications they would need to make to standard software, information on other products and services, the extent to which they work with relevant third parties, options on pricing and 'working in partnership' with your organisation. This section is key to ensuring that you get the answers to your main questions in a standard form. Having said that, even the best supplier questionnaires are mysteriously ignored by some suppliers who insist on providing you with their standard proposals, sometimes not even cross-referenced to your questions!

■ *Terms and conditions of response* – your terms of business for the tendering, including the costs of producing the tender (usually none to be borne by you), confidentiality, and key contractual terms (e.g. acceptance procedures, correction of faults and errors, reliance on suppliers' representations). You might as well find out now if some of your 'showstopper' contractual terms make you a non-starter for some of these suppliers.

Think broadly when drawing up a long list of potential suppliers. For example, if you suspect that a bespoke solution might be required, include package providers and bespoke development houses so you can compare the two approaches. Be prepared to use your imagination when considering possible packages. For example, a good commercial sales and contact management system might meet your fundraising needs. The Cancer Research Campaign, for example, chose a legal probate system for its legacies administration rather than a conventional legacies administration system.

Try to avoid having too long a long list – remember that you will need to review all the tenders you receive and that some suppliers (sometimes the better ones) will be reluctant to quote if they know that they are on a very long list. Six to twelve suppliers is a sensible rule of thumb.

Software directories, consultancy advice, word of mouth networking, magazine articles and common sense are all useful techniques in coming up with an appropriate, well-balanced tender list – you should probably use them all to maximise your chances of success.

Selection of supplier(s)

The purpose of this stage is to:

■ Reduce a long list to a short list for more detailed evaluation.
■ Enjoy learning from demonstrations and presentations.

- Start the process of 'due diligence' through references and site visits.
- Choose a preferred supplier (or two).

An ideal short list should comprise two or three suppliers, all of whom appear capable of meeting the requirements. Remember that until this point you have only tested the product fit (does the software seem to meet the requirements?). At the skills level, so far you have only tested the suppliers' ability to write proposals and produce marketing literature. You have not tested the skills you actually want to buy, i.e. the suppliers' skills at providing the services you will need to get your required benefits from the software.

The modern approach to this stage of the process is 'hands-on', with the purchaser looking carefully at the suppliers' track record and business acumen, as well as the skills and manner of their staff. Unless you are keen on slick, standard presentations, it is usually a good idea to discourage suppliers in advance from spending much time on 'talking up' their companies. Uncontrolled software demonstrations spend much of the time on glossy generalities and fail to allow enough time for the detailed discussions that might usefully cover key issues and options (i.e. what is really useful to you). Software salespeople are often highly skilled at 'selling the sizzle and not the sausage'. Software demonstrations should focus on demonstrating the suppliers' ability to meet your key and most tricky requirements.

You will often need to take a lead to ensure that the demonstration achieves your objectives. Don't be afraid to ask tough questions, questions on subjects where you might feel a bit green and especially pertinent questions to which you think you could guess the answer. For more complex, non-standard needs, you should encourage suppliers to prototype a non-standard element of your requirement to demonstrate their ability to understand and meet your needs – sometimes referred to as a 'competitive model office' test.

A competent software salesperson will be very nice to you and compliment you on the quality of your invitation to tender, your choice of fine consultants or, alternatively, your wisdom in neglecting to produce an invitation to tender and/or your wisdom in not using consultants. Some will serve you decent coffee and biscuits. You might even hit the jackpot and get lunch. These aspects test very little. When you are potentially buying services as well as product, try to insist on meeting at least one of the operational staff who will be involved in your project, not just sales (or business development) staff.

At the end of this stage, ideally you should find yourself with a preferred supplier with whom you hope to agree a contract, plus a good reserve in the wings just in case the due diligence and contracts work puts you off your preferred supplier.

Do you need help with all of this?

With large or complex applications, most not-for-profit organisations can benefit from independent help by appointing consultants. Even with smaller applications, good consultants should be prepared to help you on a modest scale, e.g. by providing some quality assurance on specification and tender documents produced by your staff, helping you to find suitable suppliers for the long list and quality assuring key decision points (e.g. shortlisting and choosing a preferred supplier). You might well also need specialist help with due diligence and contract negotiation (see below).

The use of hardware or software suppliers as consultants may result in a conflict of interests when choosing solutions, so should normally be avoided. Good consultancy help should ensure that benefits are clearly defined, the project's objectives and scope are clear, a proper methodology is followed and contracts with solution suppliers are robust enough to control the project risks.

Due diligence

The purpose of due diligence is to understand the risks inherent in proceeding with your preferred supplier – not to put some ticks in boxes on a checklist and congratulate yourself that you have completed it in record time. You should be asking hard questions at this stage and you are unlikely to get satisfactory answers to all of them. The key point is that you know what you are letting yourself in for and are able to plan around the risks and weaknesses you uncover. Above all, be prepared to walk away from a supplier who is really falling short of your required standards.

Under normal circumstances, we suggest that you only undertake the due diligence process on your preferred supplier. Occasionally, where you have a difficult choice between two suppliers, it makes sense to undertake some or all of the due diligence on both to help you with your final choice.

The following checklists set out the main aspects you should consider and show an example of the questions you might ask when following up references.

DUE DILIGENCE CHECKLIST

☑ Several telephone references from suitable clients of supplier

☑ Site visits to one or two especially suitable clients of supplier

- ☑ Visit to supplier's site(s) for support and maintenance checks
- ☑ Financial stability checks
- ☑ Quality systems checks
- ☑ Ethical checks
- ☑ Technical compatibility with your current and planned IT infrastructure
- ☑ Key technical competencies assessment
- ☑ Supplier's project management skills and methods
- ☑ Outstanding points on software functionality
- ☑ Reasonableness of supplier's profits in deal
- ☑ Full and reasonable disclosure of both parties' abilities
- ☑ Agreed policy on publicity (e.g. future references, articles)
- ☑ Appropriate sharing of risks (e.g. liability, risk transfer) in deal
- ☑ Adequate warranties from both parties to form part of deal

---

EXAMPLE QUESTIONS FOR REFERENCE CALLS AND VISITS CHECKLIST

- ☑ How long have you been working with the supplier?
- ☑ What work did the supplier do for you ?
- ☑ Why did you choose the supplier ?
- ☑ What was the competition like?
- ☑ How did the implementation go:
    - – requirements understood
    - – on time
    - – on budget
    - – data conversion successful?
- ☑ How do you use the software?
- ☑ Remote users ?
- ☑ All PCs?
- ☑ Do you do much reporting?
- ☑ Have you built your own reports?
- ☑ How much searching and querying do you do?
- ☑ Did the software meet your expectations?
- ☑ Much tailoring needed?
- ☑ Do you use the software for purposes other than those originally anticipated – if so, what purposes?
- ☑ How do you rate the tool kit?
- ☑ Were you disappointed in:

   – any element of the software
   – the project management of the implementation
   – other elements of the supplier's work
   – support and maintenance
   – documentation?

☑ Do you import/export data ?

☑ Any problems?

☑ Please describe your relationship with the supplier's staff

☑ Is there any advice you can offer us in our dealings with:
   – the supplier as a company
   – the supplier's people for implementation
   – the supplier's people for support and maintenance
   – the software itself
   – documentation and ancillary material?

☑ Other questions specific to your selection

As a minimum, you should seek several telephone references and visit one or two customer sites of similar type and/or complexity level to yourselves. However much you might be relying on trusted external consultants to help you, it is vital that key charity staff are also involved at this stage of the process – often the final decision between two equally good technical solutions comes down mainly to personalities and a greater feeling of comfort with one supplier.

Surprisingly little effort is required to take a proper look at shortlisted suppliers (e.g. a few days in more complex cases for an experienced buyer to scrutinise two or three). Remember, very few suppliers look exemplary under the microscope, but you will understand the strengths and weaknesses of the supplier before deciding to buy. Further, you can plan around any expected shortcomings and avoid unpleasant surprises.

Supplier weaknesses uncovered at this stage often include poor project management and inability to deliver projects on time and on budget. Don't just shrug your shoulders and say 'oh well' or 'shoot the messenger – they probably just didn't work well with the supplier'. Think carefully about whether you want to proceed in these circumstances. If you do, then you should consider applying resources to make up for the supplier shortfall in project management skills (e.g. through your own strong resource or through trusted external advisors). Ask the supplier to explain any shortcomings in the references. Also, make sure that you pay a great deal of attention to making the supplier think through the project plan and all the tasks they are required to deliver. Sometimes you'll find that their estimated costs and timescales increase. So be it, at least you have flushed out the truth before signing a contract. And you can always walk away from the deal if it no longer seems right for you (see 'Contract negotiation and agreement', below).

In completing your due diligence, fill in any gaps that were not adequately covered in the supplier's response to your invitation to tender. Perhaps you still need to assess their commitment to quality, e.g. does the supplier have a quality system such as ISO9000 or TickIT (the latter is the software industry's version of ISO9001) or a total quality management programme? Perhaps you still need to assess their stability (is the supplier's financial position secure, is it an imminent merger/takeover target?). Perhaps you still need to assess the supplier's appropriateness to your organisation longer term (e.g. does it have a significant, appropriate client base or share of the market?).

There are two conflicting extremes or pitfalls you should try to avoid at this stage:

- Being deadline driven to the extent that you shortcut part of the due diligence in order to meet your timetable.
- Becoming nervous about making a final decision to the extent that you protract the due diligence process or reject a supplier on the basis of a few weaknesses.

It really is not possible to provide generic guidance on the above pitfalls, simply to say that you should look out for them and try to keep a clear mind throughout.

Contract negotiation and agreement

The purpose of this stage is to:

- Beat the poor unfortunate chosen supplier into submission to your draconian and miserly contractual terms (old fashioned style) – wrong!
- Or – to reach a mutually acceptable contract that shares risks and rewards between the parties fairly, co-operatively and sensibly (the modern way) – right!
- Agree to proceed.

Even if you have a strong preference for one supplier, it nearly always makes sense to make your decision 'subject to contract' and to keep an alternative supplier in play (if there is a suitable alternative) until the contract is signed. Remember that if you do move to your reserve supplier you should complete your due diligence on that supplier if you have not already done so.

Increasingly, procurement is about imaginative contractual relationships (e.g. testing suppliers' ability to provide services to support products by making levels of support service contractual, job swapping between supplier and charity, performance related pricing). These are techniques that can help you to share the risks and rewards of this relationship fairly, co-operatively and sensibly.

While concluding your evaluation, remember that you still have the (surprisingly rarely used) option to reject all suppliers because none offers sufficient rewards to compensate you for the costs and risks inherent in the project. Don't let fancy features and fast talk make you lose sight of your objectives. It is always worth stopping and thinking before signing on the dotted line. Is the proposed solution really in line with the objectives, scope and benefits you are seeking? Is there still a business case for proceeding?

Wherever possible, you should ensure that your requirements specification forms part of your contract with the supplier, unless they are entirely standard (e.g. basic financial ledgers).

The contract should normally include a process for installation, testing, acceptance and training, clearly defining both parties' responsibilities.

When buying standard software (or even when commissioning minor modifications to standard packages), the contract will normally comprise a licence to use – you would not normally expect to own the intellectual property. If, despite all warnings to avoid this route, you are set on commissioning a bespoke solution, you should normally insist on owning the resulting intellectual property. Note that in the absence of a stated clause the software house is deemed to own the intellectual property, even though you have paid for it.

You will almost certainly require a contract for support and maintenance – this sometimes forms part of a single contract (e.g. a licence to use which includes support and upgrades) and sometimes comes separately.

In particular, you should be prepared to walk away from a supplier if you find them unwilling or unreasonable in seeing through promises or written undertakings to the level of contractual commitment. If trust between the parties has become soured at the contract negotiation stage, it is unlikely to improve as a result of your capitulation over contracts. Indeed, you are probably setting yourselves up for failure.

Before actually signing the contract, remember your initial feasibility and your objectives. Are you still going to meet enough of your original objectives? Do the benefits outweigh the costs? Are the rewards you expect from the project commensurate with the risks you are taking? Do you believe you are sufficiently geared up to manage the risks to ensure that the project succeeds? Have you completed your legal review? If the answer to any of the questions is no, either you have not really completed the selection job or there is now an inherent flaw in the original proposition. If the answer to these questions is yes, you should be ready to sign and you should have set yourselves up for a successful implementation. Good luck.

Summary

- A frightening proportion of IT projects fail to meet their objectives, a failure that can usually be attributed to a failure to follow a proper process – so don't make that mistake.
- Smaller systems choices still need a proper process, the work required to follow that proper process is just significantly less than for a large system.
- Always conduct a feasibility exercise – i.e. set out the project's scope and objectives and assess the possible costs, benefits, risks and rewards of the project – many a seemingly good idea should bite the dust at this stage.
- Specify your functional requirements – keep this short and simple unless your requirements are unusual and/or complex.
- Use an invitation to tender to whittle down your long list of suppliers (say six to twelve) to a few potential suppliers.
- Select a supplier by evaluating (probably two or three) suitable suppliers in more detail (e.g. presentations and possibly some early stages of due diligence such as telephone references).
- Use consultants to help you with the above to the extent that you need their skills (the size and complexity of your requirements and the amount of in-house expertise you have are relevant factors). Good consultants should be flexible to your needs.
- Make sure when you use professional advice for choosing solutions that the advisors are independent.
- Satisfy yourselves that you understand the risks inherent in proceeding with your chosen supplier through undertaking due diligence.
- Don't rush your decision at this stage, but also do not get bogged down and become unable to make a final decision.
- Remember that you can always walk away from a supplier at this stage if due diligence uncovers insurmountable weaknesses.
- Make sure you end up with a realistic contract that shares risks and rewards between you and the supplier fairly, co-operatively and sensibly.
- Have one final pause for thought – make sure that the whole idea still makes sense before you sign.

Implementing systems – driving home benefits

CHAPTER OBJECTIVES

In this chapter we shall:

- Emphasise the need to drive home benefits through project management (not just 'get something in on time and on budget').
- Set out a risk/reward approach to implementing systems which should help you to minimise the risks and maximise the rewards of your implementations.
- Encourage you to review your IT projects post implementation to improve the effectiveness of future projects and indeed the implementation you are reviewing.

Project managing implementation projects

In chapter 14 we set out some worrying statistics on IT project failure in order to convince you to use a proper process for selecting systems. Choosing an appropriate system minimises many project risks and helps you to plan the implementation sensibly, but it does not guarantee IT project success. Indeed, completing the systems selection is not even the beginning of the end, it is merely the end of the beginning of the project. The implementation stage of the project requires solid project management to minimise risks and maximise rewards. In our experience, the technical risks of the project are often given disproportionate attention, at the expense of longer term risks of failing to drive home the very benefits that initiated the project in the first place. 'We got the thing in on time and on budget' is an achievement in itself, but it is a bit of a 'so what?' achievement if benefits don't flow from the project.

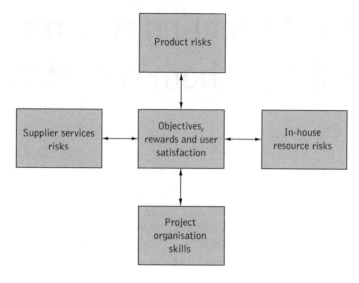

Adapted from Porter's 5 forces model

FIGURE 15.1 Project risk/reward model

The diagram above shows an IT project risk/reward model. The earlier phases of your systems project, discussed above, should already have identified the benefits (rewards) sought and several of the areas of risk.

By directing systems projects towards their potential rewards and minimising the risks along the way, you can vastly increase the likelihood of a project's success. A risk/reward management approach to project management requires clear thinking and the ability to make decisions (sometimes tough ones). It is a rigorous approach to achieving the objectives and rewards that led to you initiating the systems project in the first place. This approach is entirely in line with structured methodologies for project management, such as PRINCE 2 (often mandatory in the government sector for IT projects). We would advocate the use of structured methodologies only in large project environments (most voluntary sector IT projects are not large). In our experience, structured methodologies are sometimes used as an alternative to structured thinking; in such circumstances the methodology which aims to help the project to succeed can become the 'trees that prevent you from seeing the wood' in driving home the benefits. Nevertheless, structured methodologies are very useful when large projects involving many people need to be controlled in a standardised way. In all cases, we promote the use of clear and analytical thinking to minimise risks and maximise rewards.

Learning the lessons

George Santayana once said '...progress, far from consisting in change, depends on retentiveness ... Those who cannot remember the past are condemned to repeat it' (Santayana, 1905). Although Santayana was not referring to post implementation reviews of IT projects, his words seem pertinent in that context.

Sadly, few IT projects are evaluated post project. Exhausted, demoralised, slightly embarrassed and late starting the next project, often there just isn't time. This is a pity. Evaluation is a valuable way of learning from our successes and our mistakes in order to allow continuous improvement. A post project review can also produce substantial benefits to the project itself:

- Assessment of whether objectives have been met and rewards gained – also a means of deciding what additional activities, if any, are required to meet those objectives and gain those rewards.
- Appraising user satisfaction (or lack thereof) – often some early feedback can identify issues which can relatively easily improve the user's longer term perception of the success of the project and of their satisfaction.
- Identifying learning points for future projects – given the consistently high failure rates of IT projects, it seems a shame that organisations are not learning from their mistakes. We suggest that solid risk/reward assessment post project would go some way to improving the track record for IT projects.

For larger projects, the post project review is a small project in itself, but for smaller projects a brief assessment addressing the above points would achieve many of the benefits sought from evaluation.

Risk/reward activity from choosing through to post implementation review

Table 15.1 overleaf shows a sensible pattern of risk/reward activity divided between the phases of an IT systems project. It is not exhaustive, but should illustrate many of the principles involved and provide checklists for you at each stage of your selection and implementation work.

TABLE 15.1 IT project risk/reward management

Areas of risk and reward	IT project management phase or stage		
	Planning (choosing process from business case through to selection)	Implementation (driving home benefits)	Evaluation (learning and continuous improvement)
Objectives, rewards and user satisfaction	■ Define objectives ■ Estimate rewards	■ Set objectives and rewards as goals ■ Manage user expectations ■ Seek early wins to prove user benefits and start virtuous spiral	■ Have the objectives been met? ■ Have the rewards been gained? ■ Have unintended rewards been found? ■ Are the users satisfied?
Product risks	■ General knowledge of IT product market place ■ Compare IT product risks between potential solutions	■ Plan management of foreseen product risks ■ Revise project plans to manage down emerging product risks	■ Does the product perform? ■ Can it be enhanced or modified?
Supplier services risks	■ General knowledge of IT supplier market place ■ Compare supplier risks between potential solutions	■ Plan management of foreseen supplier risks ■ Revise project plans to manage emerging supplier risks	■ Did the supplier perform during implementation? ■ What have we learned for our ongoing relationship with the supplier?
In-house resources risks	■ Part of risk assessment for feasibility ■ Risks clarify as scope of project and in-house resource requirements clarify	■ Required resources include IT infrastructure, technical skills (often IT, financial and operational), experience of implementing systems ■ Trade-off between other calls on in-house resources and this systems project ■ Ensure that you have planned, budgeted for and scheduled sufficient training and skills transfer	■ Are our resources appropriate for projects like this? ■ What else have we learned for future projects?
Project organisation risks	■ Outline success metrics from objectives and predicted rewards	■ Defined roles, responsibilities and reporting lines ■ Defined project milestones ■ Project control ■ Project monitoring and evaluation	■ Did we manage the project well? ■ What have we learnt to help us manage projects better in future?

Summary

- Ensure that you manage your IT projects to drive home the benefits you sought in the first place.
- Concentrate on minimising risks and maximising rewards from your implementation.
- Make the time to evaluate your IT projects, for the sake of both those projects themselves and for your future IT projects.

Part 4

IT staff, skills and style

IT staff, skills and style – using this part

This part covers the 'softer' aspects of applying IT to the not-for-profit sector, such as human resources. It is a mixture of reflective advice and pragmatic tips. Most applies to not-for-profit organisations of all shapes and sizes. The initial chapter, 'The Four Cs', sets out principles which we believe to be extremely important in achieving results when applying IT in any environment. Similarly, 'Sensible use of consultants' and 'Training and skills transfer' should be useful to all.

People interested in larger not-for-profit organisations should benefit from reading all the chapters in this part. Chapter 19, 'Outsourcing', is likely to be useful only in organisations large enough to justify dedicated IT staff, although the principles set out in the chapter might apply to outsourcing aspects of your undertakings other than IT.

People interested in smaller and medium-sized not-for-profit organisations might be especially concerned with chapter 20, 'Technophobia and technoscepticism'. These issues can be crucial, especially if one or two key individuals in a smaller organisation show these characteristics. However, we believe the messages in that chapter to be useful and applicable to all manner of organisations.

The four Cs

CHAPTER OBJECTIVES

In this chapter we shall:

- Recognise that successful IT in non-profit organisations is at least as much down to people as it is to technology.
- Explain the four Cs that we believe help people to succeed in their IT planning, implementation and evaluation: communication, contribution, consensus and commitment.
- Emphasise the need to document your Cs.
- Provide some tips and techniques to help you use those four Cs.

The human touch

We have described earlier the benefits of communicating and gathering contributions from your staff when planning IT and procuring systems. Despite the increasing importance of information technology, not-for-profit organisations are (and will continue to be) essentially people businesses. In fact all organisations, especially service-based ones, are people businesses.

Further, however good your IT systems and structure might be, they are unlikely to deliver the benefits you hoped for unless your staff have both the skills and the motivation to deliver the benefits. Or put another way, if there is an absence of motivation it is extremely unlikely that an IT project will succeed.

We believe that the motivation to deliver benefits, i.e. commitment to any IT project or initiative, stems from:

- *Communication* with people about the project or initiative.
- Gathering *contributions* from those people at the planning, implementation and evaluation stages.
- Trying to build *consensus* on the appropriate course of action.

All of these usually lead to *commitment*.

This is not a naïve view that not-for-profit organisations can please all the people all the time with IT projects, but an application of wide experience that says that a sensible level of engagement with people who will be affected by IT projects significantly increases the prospects of success.

Document as you go

Personnel changes often have adverse effects on IT projects, from both the skills and motivation point of view and may result in your project having a skills gap at a vital time. Further, new people coming in, having not been involved in the initial communications and contributions, can take a negative attitude to the project. 'Not invented here' manifests itself in phrases such as 'well I wouldn't have done it this way'. One way to minimise these risks is to make sure you document your work as you go. It is harder (though not impossible) for a new person to be ultra critical of the decisions made if there is evidence that they have been clearly thought through and agreed by consensus. Although such documentation is not quite the same thing as having been involved in the process, it does help people to buy in part way through. Further, such documentation should help a new person to get up to speed that much quicker. It is worth investing time in face-to-face briefing and discussion with new people who will have key roles in projects, to let them air any concerns and ensure understanding through dialogue.

On any project or venture, especially if it is IT related, you should periodically ask yourself the question 'if [so and so] fell under a bus tomorrow, would anyone be able to see this project through?' If the answer is no, you probably need that person to document what they are doing more thoroughly and possibly ought to ensure that someone else works with them sufficiently to be able to provide some cover if the worst happens.

Where do I start to be a good four Cs player?

The table below sets out a checklist of communication, contribution and consensus activities which you should think about for each project.

TABLE 16.1 Communication contribution and consensus checklist			
Project stage	**Communication**	**Contribution**	**Consensus**
Plan ('think and tell')	■ Have you alerted all relevant people to the IT project idea? ■ Have you formulated a communication plan for the ensuing project?	■ Have you consulted with people who will be directly affected by the IT project idea? ■ Have you consulted with a sample of those who will be indirectly affected? ■ Have you documented that consultation?	■ Have you allowed a proper airing for alternative proposals? ■ Have you ensured that a suitable proportion of people agree with the proposal? ■ Have you documented those debates, including options you have considered but rejected?
Implement ('act')	■ Are you communicating regularly about this IT project (e.g. newsletters, global e-mails, briefings)? ■ Are you taking steps to gauge the effectiveness of your communication?	■ Are you getting contributions from people for the project as planned? ■ Are new people being included in the contribution plan? ■ Is there a mechanism for wider contributions (e.g. feedback questionnaires)?	■ Is there a mechanism for error logging, complaints and suggestions? ■ Have you set up mechanisms for shared learning (e.g. meetings, bulletin boards)?
Evaluate ('improve and share')	■ Are you 'publishing' (internally) the results of and comments on the project? ■ Have you considered wider publication (beyond your organisation)?	■ Has 'customer satisfaction' been assessed (e.g. through a questionnaire, evaluation meeting or call)? ■ Have you conducted a post implementation review? ■ Have you publicised the results of these evaluations?	■ Are shared learning mechanisms being used by users? ■ Have you set up channels for 'where do we go from here' dialogue? ■ Are you sure people have been told how to share their knowledge?

Summary

■ IT projects are far more likely to succeed with committed people.

■ Communication, contribution and consensus usually lead to commitment.

■ Document your activities as you go to maximise your chances of success even if key people on the project change part way through.

Sensible use of consultants

CHAPTER OBJECTIVES

In this chapter we shall:

- Sketch out various consultancy roles and commend some of them.
- Try to be objective, given that we are consultants who aspire to be used sensibly.
- Set out some consultancy industry guidelines.
- Interpret those guidelines for use of consultants in the not-for-profit sector.

Consultancy roles

We need to declare a potential conflict of interest before discussing the sensible use of consultants. We are both directors of Z/Yen Limited which is a risk/reward management practice. One of our specialisms is to provide strategic, process and IT systems consultancy for the not-for-profit sector. This specialism at the time of writing accounts for about 25 per cent of our advisory business. We nevertheless feel qualified and able to advise the reader on the sensible use of consultants.

There are four consultancy roles commonly used by not-for-profit organisations:

- Body shopping.
- Strategy consultation.
- Organisational fool.
- Process consultant or specialist.

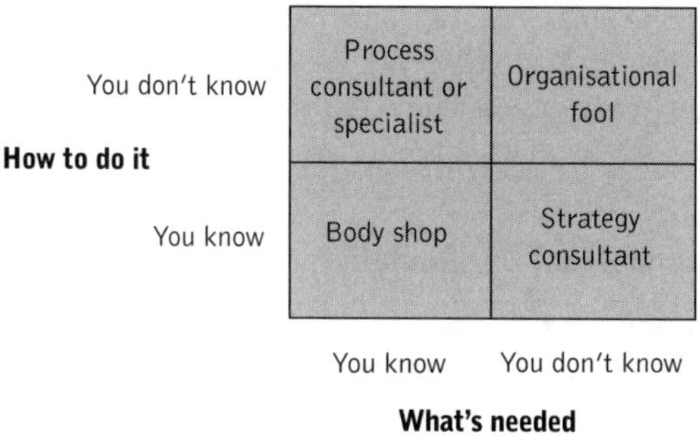

FIGURE 17.1 Consultancy roles

Body shopping

When you know what you need to do and you know how to do it, but use third party 'consultancy' help anyway. In other words, you are merely overcoming resourcing problems by using consultants. In certain specialist areas (IT, at times, being one of them) this might be the only way you can find an appropriately skilled resource. However, as we argue in this and the next chapter, we believe that not-for-profit organisations should seek to minimise this type of use of consultants. This is best achieved by ensuring that sufficient people are trained and able to use the IT. There are times when the use of resources in this way is unavoidable, indeed the current authors' practice, Z/Yen, makes a fair proportion of its living this way. However, we believe that body-shopping is only a sensible use of consultants in the short term. We encourage clients, especially in the not-for-profit sector, to acquire medium to long term self-sufficiency as quickly as possible.

Strategy consultant

When you don't know what is needed, but would know how to get it done once you knew. This can be a sensible use of consultants, and not-for-profit organisations will often sensibly engage in medium to long term (but far from full time and therefore relatively inexpensive) relationships with consultants to provide strategic input at key times and/or in key places. In the IT area, this tends to manifest itself in the form of strategies or strategic reviews of specific aspects of an organisation's IT.

Organisational fool

When you neither know what is needed nor how to do it, and choose to use a consultant to find out. Occasionally it can be useful to get a third party to 'hold a mirror up to your organisation's face' and help you to generate ideas. Indeed, some large corporate organisations often use consultants in this way. We believe that this use of consultants can only be sensible for not-for-profit organisations short term.

Process consultant or specialist

When you know what is needed but don't know how to do it. This is probably the most common use of IT consultants in the not-for-profit sector. Not-for-profit organisations will often sensibly engage in medium to long term (but not extensive) relationships with con-

TABLE 17.1 Institute of Management Consultancy guidelines for choosing and using management consultants

IMC golden rule	IMC notes	Authors' comments
1 Clearly define the objectives that you hope to achieve	■ Describe the job you want done and specify the things you expect from the assignment. ■ Understand precisely how you expect your business will benefit from the work. ■ Decide on the timescales, scope and any constraints on the assignment. ■ Clarify your own role, which key staff will be involved, and how their time will be made available.	■ Benefits might not always be measurable in financial terms, but you should nevertheless seek to define tangible success measures ■ Having unclear terms of reference is one of the most common reasons for not-for-profits' relationships with consultants to go wrong ■ Although good consultants should help you to define the objectives and scope, the onus is on you to ensure that they are appropriate for your organisation
2 Consult with others in your organisation to agree those objectives	■ Consult with appropriate fellow directors and managers on the nature of the problem. ■ Jointly define your specific needs for the expertise you want. Is it a systems, human or skills problem? ■ You may decide that you require regular 'hand holding' discussions or counselling sessions with the management consultant rather than a defined assignment. Many clients obtain considerable value from scheduling assistance in this way – but make sure you still have a written fee quote and terms of reference.	■ The 'hand holding' discussions approach is often an appropriate one for not-for-profit organisations with limited budgets and a desire or need for skills transfer ■ Normally not-for-profit organisations should avoid 'handing an entire problem over' to consultants. Although this might seem a good way to solve short-term resourcing problems, it can often lead to the relationship becoming protracted and therefore unnecessarily excessively expensive
3 Short-list no more than three consultants, and ask them to provide written proposals	■ Make sure you ask only such consultants to quote for the work as are qualified to carry it out. The Institute of Management consultancy has a code of conduct which requires its members not to take on assignments for which they are not qualified.	■ Not-for-profit organisations often assume that the consultants require a great deal of experience in their organisation's specialised field, whereas usually you do not need that experience from the consultant, as you have that specialist knowledge yourselves

TABLE 17.1 Institute of Management Consultancy guidelines for choosing and using management consultants [continued]

IMC golden rule	IMC notes	Authors' comments

	■ If you do not know a suitable consultant, ask the Institute Of Management Consultancy (IMC). We run a free client support service that can put you in contact with a number of qualified consultants or consultancy practices. Potential consultants will be happy to send you basic information about themselves and talk with you about your needs, without charge.
	■ Invite the consultancies identified by IMC to submit written proposals, which should include:
	  – their understanding of the problem
	  – the brief
	  – name(s) and CV(s) of the consultant(s) who will do the work
	  – experience of the firm
	  – references
	  – other support provided by the firm,
	  – work plan and timeshare – reports and/or systems that will be supplied to you
	  – fees, expenses and schedules of payment
	  – the inputs required from you.
		■ We believe it is beneficial to not-for-profit organisations that the chosen providers of consultancy expertise have significant experience working in both the voluntary sector and other sectors, so that the consultants understand the culture and financial constraints of the voluntary sector while providing you with a breadth of skills and experience

4 Brief the consultants properly	■ Prepare a concise brief which clearly defines the objectives, scope, timescale, reporting procedure and constraints of the project and agree it with others in your organisation who will have an influence on the outcome of the project. ■ Remember that the cheapest quote will not necessarily give the best value for money, and the fees of your preferred consultant(s) may be negotiable.	■ Do not compare costs solely on day rates, but also consider defined benefits (what outputs are you going to get for your money?) and quality (people who take three times as long to do a task are often not the highest quality people for that task) ■ Ensure that you agree a fixed maximum fee or at least a capped budget for a defined scope of work
5 See the individual consultant who will do the job and make sure that the 'chemistry' is right	■ Successful consultancy requires goodwill in human communications. Meet the consultant(s) who will be doing the job and brief them well, using the written brief and any background information that you or they think necessary. ■ Talk through your chosen proposal with the consultant before making a final decision to ensure that you have any concerns answered. If you are not happy with any aspects of the proposal	■ It is sadly common for not-for-profit organisations to see only a principal of the consultancy during the consultancy sales process ■ In our experience, not-for-profit organisations should usually expect a principal to be providing 10 to 25 per cent of the consultancy effort involved ■ Last minute team changes are an occasional fact of life, even from the best practices – your organisation

TABLE 17.1 Institute of Management Consultancy guidelines for choosing and using management consultants [continued]

IMC golden rule	IMC notes	Authors' comments
	do not feel pressured into accepting them. Continue discussions with the consultant until full agreement on the proposal can be reached. ■ Select the firm or individual that you feel has the best qualifications and experience and who you feel you can work with comfortably.	should nevertheless have a right to vet and veto rather than have team changes imposed upon you ■ Working with sole practitioner consultants is often appropriate for not-for-profit organisations, but do bear in mind the risks inherent in relying on just one person
6 Ask for references from the chosen consultant(s) and follow them up	■ Ask the firm or individual chosen for names or written references from former clients in order to verify the consultants' suitability for the assignment.	■ The not-for-profit world is a fairly close-knit community and reference taking often takes place informally, nevertheless it makes sense as a courtesy and to help your evaluation to agree referees formally with the chosen consultant to ensure that you are taking references on appropriate assignments and consultancy staff
7 Review and agree a written contract before the assignment starts	(there are no notes appended to this golden rule)	■ Be more than a little wary of working with a consultant or consultancy that seems indifferent to this golden rule ■ Work at the document – each word means something
8 Be involved and in touch during the assignment	■ Using consultants effectively demands a commitment of time as well as money by clients. ■ Remember that you must keep in touch with the progress of the assignment if you are to get the most from it. Consultants are likely to be most cost-effective when working to an agreed programme and timescale. Make sure there are regular progress meetings and that the consultant keeps you fully briefed on progress against the programme. ■ To implement the recommendations it is often most cost-effective to involve the consultant(s) together with your management. ■ If you and your staff need to provide input, make sure that you do it within the agreed timescale. Extra costs may be incurred if you hold up the progress of the assignment. Consultancy requires an investment not only in fees but also in client time. ■ Assignments are usually most effective when the work is done on the client's premises. Make sure you can provide suitable office space and administrative support for the consultants.	■ Mercifully, in our experience not-for-profit organisations rarely try to 'throw money at problems' by 'chucking projects over a fence for consultants to deal with' ■ A relationship between a not-for-profit organisation and a consultancy should be a partnership-style 'two way street' rather than an antagonistic customer-supplier showdown – in our experience not-for-profit organisations tend to be good at working this way as long as the consultancy is appropriately equipped to work co-operatively

TABLE 17.1 Institute of Management Consultancy guidelines for choosing and using management consultants [continued]		
IMC golden rule	**IMC notes**	**Authors' comments**
	■ You should aim to involve your staff in the assignment as early as possible so that they partly 'own' the recommendations and have an interest in the results. ■ Assignments are often most effective when run by a joint team of consultants and staff and when the contents of the consultant's report are agreed with the staff at a progress meeting.	
9 Ensure that the consultant does not save surprises for the final report	■ The consultant's report is often his or her most tangible 'deliverable', but it must be in a format which is beneficial to you. If necessary, ask the consultant to produce a draft report so that you can discuss findings and recommendations with some of your colleagues before the final report is produced. ■ The final report should contain no surprises. If there are very confidential or contentious issues, ask for these to be put into a private letter rather than in the report itself. Make sure the report is written in a way you and your staff can understand and use. Tell the consultant if you are not happy with it. ■ Ask the consultant to make a presentation to you and your colleagues, if this will help discussion on its conclusions. ■ You should note, however, that some assignments will not result in a written report. If this is the case, make sure you understand what the 'deliverable' will be before the assignment starts.	■ Not-for-profit organisations probably more than most sectors benefit from an 'iterative' approach to producing reports (as described in this rule) ■ It is often appropriate to agree a report outline with the consultants before they produce a draft report, to ensure that the report is fit for your purpose – such a report outline sometimes forms part of the consultants' proposal. ■ Not-for-profit organisations usually need and seek pragmatic help from consultants, so do make sure that final reports contain a significant amount of 'action plan', 'next steps' and 'way forward' material to help you implement the recommendations – such material is often sensibly withheld from early drafts so that action plans are only produced once recommendations are agreed
10 Implement the recommendations and involve your management as well as the consultant	■ You may need to make arrangements for the management consultant to help with the implementation. This can be done cost-effectively by involving the consultant in regular progress meetings. Get a written fee quotation and proposal for any implementation work, even if it follows directly from an assignment	■ Not-for-profit organisations sometimes skimp in this area to their cost, but often you will find that a little help can go a long way to ensure that the vision and key recommendations are implemented sensibly ■ However you decide to resource the implementation of recommendations, you should at least always have a good deep think to ensure that you are applying appropriate resources to get things done

sultants to provide specialist IT and/or process input at key times. This type of use often manifests itself in using consultants to help with the scoping, specification, tendering, evaluation and selection of systems. It also tends to encompass project management and/or quality assurance of implementations, post implementation reviews, IT resource studies and IT financial planning.

Choosing and using consultants sensibly

To give this part of the chapter an acceptable level of independence, we shall in large part rely on Institute of Management Consultancy (IMC) guidelines (published with permission below), which set out ten golden rules for choosing and using consultants (both sole practitioners and consultancy practices) effectively.

Summary

- Make sure that objectives, scope and terms of the consultancy are appropriate, clear and in writing.
- Ensure that you like and have confidence in the individuals you will be working with on the consultancy project.
- Try to maximise the long-term benefits from the use of consultants to your organisation through skills transfer and handover planning.

Training and skills transfer

CHAPTER OBJECTIVES

In this chapter we shall:

- Encourage you to ensure that training is high on your agenda when planning IT projects.
- Explain why skills transfer is so important, especially for not-for-profit organisations.
- Provide tips on appropriate training and skills transfer.

Catch the training

Most people wouldn't dream of getting into a car and driving without first having driving lessons. Most managers wouldn't dream of letting an untrained clerk loose on their accounts. Yet somehow many people take a 'Heath Robinson' approach to IT and assume that they and others will be able to muddle through. And this despite the fact that the equipment and systems are at least as difficult to navigate and use as the car and double entry book-keeping.

Many of us have been guilty of this mistake at times, as the case example on the next page testifies.

Some people need the discipline and peer group you get with classroom training in order to learn. Others find a short burst of one-to-one training with an expert far more efficient and cost effective than standard classroom training. Some people need a combination of the above. Ideally, you should try to tailor training to individual needs and preferences as much as possible, although sometimes this is limited by budgets and timetables.

CASE EXAMPLE Confessions of Ian Harris

When, as a trainee accountant, I first encountered spreadsheets, I was self-taught and proud of it. After all, the Lotus (version 1) manual was OK-ish. Management accounting, budgeting and cash flow forecasting for small membership organisations and occupational charities formed a fairly large chunk of this work and was my first foray into the not-for-profit world. I was manipulating numbers in ways I had been quite unable to do before and ways that were impressing others. So what was training going to do for me? I eventually decided to go on an advanced spreadsheet users course in the hope of picking up some tips and some 'already half done spreadsheet models' which I thought might speed me up.

I did learn a lot from the course. Not only the stuff I expected to learn, but I learnt that some of my self-taught techniques were comparatively long winded. I realised very quickly on that course that if I had subjected myself to some training sooner, the time and money invested in the training would have been recouped many times over within months through the extra efficiency in my use of spreadsheets. Lesson learnt.

However naturally talented we might (or might not) be, some formal training is usually a good idea. Different people learn well in different ways. I am good at training from printed material and found that later versions of Lotus probably provided enough training manuals and training spreadsheet models for me to have picked up what I needed from those rather than from classroom training.

You have a huge variety of training sources to choose from. There is a competitive market place for training in standard office tool kits. The same sources we set out for finding software suppliers in chapter 14 – directories, consultancy advice, word of mouth networking, magazine articles and common sense – apply to finding potential trainers. When buying specialist package software (e.g. a fundraising system), it is usually sensible to use the supplier as your source of training and to evaluate their ability to train in that specialised software as part of your decision to buy.

Almost all of us, if we are being honest, need to get out of our own office environment to stand any chance of training in any meaningful sense of the word. For some, being in someone else's office within their own office building, with a moratorium on interruptions is enough; others need to be in a completely different building.

Why is skills transfer so important to not-for-profits?

A key aspect of making progress with IT is to ensure that sufficient skills are transferred to your organisation. 'Sufficient skills' in this context can probably be defined as those your organisation will need on a regular and/or ongoing basis. 'Skills transfer' means learning from your expert consultants and IT companies during the planning, implementation and evaluation stages of IT projects, to enable your organisation to benefit from the project on an ongoing basis without constant recourse to the external experts.

Many of the relevant points have been made in earlier chapters. Skills transfer is vital in all sectors, but especially so for cash-strapped not-for-profit organisations, which almost certainly cannot afford to or should not rely on consultants and software houses for day-to-day skills on an ongoing basis.

The problem for many not-for-profit managers is deciding which skills are 'one-off' or occasional use and which are the continuous or ongoing ones you really need in-house. Good consultants and IT companies should advise you on this, but remember that such people can have a vested interest in a continuing income stream from your organisation, so you will need to be proactive in working with your trusted advisors to plan sensible transitions.

Despite your organisation's sensible desire for self-sufficiency, you should want to maintain good, long-term relationships with good consultants and IT companies. The following points might help you to find the right balance:

- *Self-sufficiency should not extend as far as self-support*: you should almost always have support contracts in place to ensure that core systems and equipment are maintained.
- *Self-sufficiency should not extend as far as 'help yourself'*: very rarely does it make sense for a not-for-profit organisation to entice a consultant or technician away from their expert employer. Apart from the obvious moral issues, this is rarely a good idea for the organisation, IT company or the member of staff concerned. The organisation will rarely acquire a star this way. Even if the person appears to be a star, many of the skills you think you are acquiring probably accrue from that person's ongoing training and development programme with the IT company, which will stop once they work for you. Further, an otherwise good relationship between the IT company and the not-for-profit organisation might be soured by the transaction. Very occasionally such a transfer does make sense for all parties, but it should be seen as the exception rather than the rule and handled very openly, honestly and carefully.
- *Find ways of keeping in touch with your preferred suppliers*: these can include planned periodic reviews, involvement on advisory groups, social/semi-social contact, draw-down contracts for use of skills, ad hoc mini evaluations, etc. Especially in the

early stages after a large project, some of these ideas can be cost-effective ways of 'hedging your bets' on skills transfer.

Getting training and skills transfer right

Below are some tips that should help you plan training and skills transfer.

- *Ensure that an appropriate amount of training is budgeted for and scheduled as part of an IT implementation project:*
  - take soundings from organisations when you take up references to get a feel for appropriate amounts of training
  - take into account your staff's existing skills (for example, a member of staff who has regularly used a fundraising software package is likely to need less training on a new fundraising package than someone who has never used a computer before)
  - if you think the supplier might be proposing more training than you need, it often makes sense to budget for the levels of training they recommend while only committing to the amount of training you think you need, leaving the balance of training on a 'draw-down' basis to be used if needed – with some suppliers you might pay a small premium for draw-down training but a small premium can be a fair price for flexibility.
- *Tailor training to suit individuals' needs as much as is practicable:*
  - different people can have vastly different skill levels prior to training
  - different people learn in different ways
  - one of the benefits of being a smaller organisation is that you ought to be able to tailor training quite considerably without being accused of being wasteful, as there are only limited economies of scale to be had from standardisation
  - once staff have acquired a basic level of skill with a standard software package, it is often far more time and cost effective for a trainer to work with your staff on specific problems, rather than scheduling full-scale expert user courses which might only spend 10 per cent of the time covering areas relevant to your organisation
  - tailored training can actually be very cost effective, as the on-the-job training is often best achieved by actually doing the tasks in hand
  - larger not-for-profit organisations can also benefit from this principle, although we accept that an element of standardisation is needed to ensure that systems are used in a harmonised way.

- *Self-help is often the best help:*
  - we encourage many organisations, especially not-for-profits, to establish 'super-users' or 'champions' for particular packages, to help provide top-up training and encourage self-help within the organisation
  - self-help partly takes the form of surgeries where users can exchange common issues and problems – often you will find that a member of staff has laboured away for ages trying to solve an irritating IT problem that someone else has already solved
  - self-help should not be used as a substitute for formal training, but it can supplement formal training most effectively and can reduce the need for formal top-up training. It can also help in bringing new staff partly up to speed prior to their receiving formal training.
- *Assess training needs right from the start and regularly them:*
  - consider IT training needs when hiring and do not shirk from assessing them as part of the recruitment process
  - not-for-profit organisations can often acquire potentially excellent staff by selecting staff who need and seek specific training – this can form part of the deal – for example, with a starting salary below the level normally expected for the job, but with commitments from the organisation to spending money on training and from the recruit to invest time and effort in acquiring skills
  - IT training is no different from your other training needs – it should be considered along with other training needs as part of your organisation's commitment to its staff through training needs analysis.
- *Seek skills transfer when working with consultants and/or IT companies:*
  - although it is unrealistic to expect to acquire all the consultant's and/or IT company's skills 'by osmosis', your organisation should seek as much as possible to learn from the advice you receive and plan towards increasing self-sufficiency over time
  - you should state your aim towards reasonable levels of self-sufficiency up front and build appropriate mechanisms into your work programme with the advisor
  - be wary of advisors who seem unwilling to co-operate in a transfer of skills to your organisation.

Summary

- Regardless of talent (or lack of it), we can all benefit from IT training at times.

- Different people benefit from different forms of training and ideally training should be tailored to individual needs as much as possible.
- Not-for-profit organisations should seek to transfer day-to-day skills from expert advisors and IT companies.
- Getting the right balance between self-sufficiency and appropriate use of external experts can be difficult, but there are ways you can hedge your bets and it is in your organisation's interests to try and get this balance as best you can.

Outsourcing

CHAPTER OBJECTIVES

In this chapter we shall:

- Consider the aspects of IT a not-for-profit organisation might choose to outsource.
- Reflect on the general pros and cons of outsourcing.
- Provide some tips on the process you might use to outsource your IT function.
- Set out principles of service levels relevant whether or not you are outsourcing.

Outsourcing aspects

Outsourcing can be an emotive term. Say the word to some people and they immediately think of braying yuppie consultants, nightmarish uncertainty and job losses. In fact, more or less everyone uses outsourcing to some extent, so it is all a matter of degree. How many not-for-profit organisations do you know that retain their own staff to maintain IT equipment? Most organisations 'outsource' the engineering aspects of their IT to a specialist third party. We have already talked about using third parties for maintenance, support and managed facilities (see chapter 8).

Not-for-profit organisations can in fact consider outsourcing many aspects of their IT, including comprehensive outsourcing of IT – see table 19.1.

TABLE 19.1 Aspects of outsourcing

Aspect of IT	Options	Comments/matters to consider
IT strategic management/ standards	■ Consultants ■ Interim managers ■ System suppliers	■ Potential conflict of interests where comprehensive outsourcer or system supplier is involved with informing strategy or choosing solutions
IT project management	■ Comprehensive outsourcing suppliers	■ Consider the extent to which your need is short-term or medium to long-term
IT procurement		
Systems analysis and development		
IT training		
Systems support	■ Contractors ■ System suppliers	■ Usually medium to long-term arrangements
Helpdesk/ front line support	■ Facilities management suppliers ■ Comprehensive outsourcing suppliers	■ Relatively easy to compare costs and judge value for money
Operations, network and communications management		
Business process (or 'comprehensive') outsourcing	■ Comprehensive outsourcing suppliers	■ Are you able to compare costs and quality in order to evaluate value for money? ■ Is the supplier prepared to share risks and rewards with you in a fair and reasonable way?

Pros and cons

Much recent thinking on the case for outsourcing (not just in the IT arena) has hinged on whether the function you are considering outsourcing is core or non-core to your organisation. Some people use the glib phrase 'core or chore' – core being matters you want to do as they are central to your organisation's objectives, chore being those you have to get done in order to be able to do the core work. This separation is a little simplistic. Outside the IT arena, consider two not-for-profit organisations with similar revenues and operating in more or less the same field: The Cancer Research Campaign (the Campaign) and Imperial Cancer Research Fund (Imperial). The Campaign provides grants to various scientific institutions to further research into cancer. Imperial runs several research institutions, which are funded from the fund's charitable revenues. Cancer research is core to both organisations, but at a strategic level the Campaign has chosen largely to outsource the research work whereas Imperial has chosen to retain the research in house. There are perfectly

	Unacceptable	Acceptable
Capable	Core – retain	Cost/benefit decisions of outsourcing
Not capable	Build capability/ outsource acceptable bits	Chore – outsource

FIGURE 19.1 Outsourcing

valid strategic reasons for each of these approaches, but the decision certainly goes beyond the 'core or chore' division.

We therefore suggest a slightly more sophisticated analysis based on four main types of function rather than two. Consider two questions:

- Is our not-for-profit organisation capable or not so capable in the function being considered?
- Is it acceptable (e.g. strategically and/or possibly in terms of public scrutiny) for this function to be outsourced by our not-for-profit organisation?

This four-way split is still a simplification, of course. The answers to these two questions can place your organisation, or portions of it, in one of four categories. Figure 19.1, above, illustrates this thinking.

- If your organisation is highly capable in the area in question and it would be mostly unacceptable to outsource that function, it is core to your organisation and you should almost certainly retain the function in-house.
- If your organisation is highly capable in the area in question but it would be mostly acceptable to outsource the function, the decision on outsourcing should be a matter of cost/benefit analysis.
- If your organisation has low capability in the function in question and it would be mostly unacceptable to outsource that function, you need to beef up your capability and/or consider partial outsourcing (of the acceptable elements).
- If your organisation has low capability in the function in question and it would be mostly acceptable to outsource the function, there is a strong case for outsourcing it.

In chapter 8, we noted that it is hard for smaller not-for-profit organisations to find good IT service suppliers to take an interest in them and suggested more comprehensive solutions as a way of attracting better service. However, for smaller organisations on very modest budgets, it is hard to find good suppliers who will look after a small organisation well. We advocate a fair degree of self-help to such organisations. If your organisation requires a reasonable level of complexity to the solution (e.g. a client-server network and remote access services for a multi-site operation and/or for home office workers), you are likely to need a reasonable amount of IT services anyway and should at least consider outsourcing.

Some tips on the outsourcing process

The basic process for an outsourcing project is more or less the same as we advocate for other IT projects (see chapter 14):

- Agree objectives and scope in a short feasibility exercise.
- Specify your requirements in sufficient detail for an invitation to tender.
- Invite several suppliers to tender.
- Select a preferred supplier, subject to contract negotiations and transition planning.
- Agree contracts and transition plan.
- Implement the outsourcing.
- Evaluate the transition project.
- Monitor the supplier's performance on an ongoing basis (but the skills and measures required to manage complex service supplier performance are different from those required to manage a product supplier – see below).

The functions you might wish to consider outsourcing include:

- IT administration (e.g. procurement, network administration, inventory management).
- IT help desk.
- Network services (e.g. installation, server management, client-server services, disaster recovery).
- Desktop services (e.g. configuration management, office moves, hardware problems)
- Telecoms services (e.g. wide area network services, voice mail).
- Contract management (e.g. managing third party contracts, service level agreements and key performance indicator reporting for the outsourcing).

If you have staff assigned or allocated to the function which you wish to outsource, you need to take account of the TUPE (Transfer of Undertakings (Protection of Employment) Regulations). We shall not attempt to set out all the details on these complex regulations here. Suffice to say that if an undertaking or part of an undertaking is being transferred, you are legally required to transfer the relevant employees to the contractor together with their existing terms and conditions and accrued rights preserved. Terminating employment without following the TUPE regulations is by definition an unfair dismissal. The question of whether an employee is assigned or allocated to the IT function, especially in not-for-profit organisations where such roles often form a small part of several people's work activities, is unclear. You should seek professional advice in this aspect of outsourcing if you are unsure of your position, especially if you think redundancies might arise.

It is also important that you ensure that your relationship with the contractor contains appropriate escalation procedures and change control processes to enable you properly to manage the outsourcing contract once it is in place.

Possibly the biggest mistake you can make with outsourcing is to assume that you are able to outsource all aspects of the management of the function. Naturally, you can outsource the day-to-day management of your IT functions, but you cannot outsource the management of the outsourcing contract. Managing a complex contract requires different skills from those needed to manage staff. Even the better suppliers will walk all over you unless you put some effort into ensuring that you get the service you want. For example, you can outsource the day to day management of your IT security, but your policies on information security and data protection need to be your organisation's. You are simply choosing to use a contractor to implement these policies for you. Naturally, a good contractor should be able to help you with boiler plate policies which they are comfortable about enforcing for you, but your organisation needs to sign off the policies. The ultimate responsibility for your organisation remains with you.

Service levels and key performance indicators

A service department such as IT should have agreed service levels and measures against which the department is being measured, regardless of whether it is outsourced. The following guidance might equally well be applied to an in-house IT department.

Agreements should specify the service levels required and key performance indicators. In particular, when specifying requirements for an outsourcing tender, you need to pay attention to the quality or level of service you require. For example, if you are considering an outsourced IT help desk function, you need to think about service levels such as:

- The hours of service (e.g. 9.00 am to 6.00 pm).
- Your base level call waiting time (e.g. no more than fifteen seconds).
- The percentage of calls that you require to be answered within the base level call waiting time (e.g. 95 per cent).

- The manner in which you require such calls to be logged (e.g. assign and issue log numbers to all calls).
- The percentage of calls you expect to be successfully concluded at first port of call (e.g. 40 per cent).
- The frequency of reporting you expect for the above service levels (e.g. monthly).

For each function you are considering outsourcing, you will need to think about detailed service levels like those listed above. The absolute values (e.g. 95 per cent of calls answered within fifteen seconds) do not need to be agreed prior to contract time, but you do need to state that you expect these factors to form part of the contract. Nevertheless you will want to negotiate detailed service levels into the contractual relationship.

A typical service level agreement might have ten to twenty key performance indicators against which the supplier or department is being measured. Some might be absolute (e.g. no more than two unscheduled server downtime incidents per month), some percentages (e.g. a rolling average of 99 per cent network uptime during contracted hours). Service level agreements often also contain some qualitative measures of user satisfaction, probably measured by a sampling survey (e.g. at least 60 per cent of users should be satisfied or very satisfied with the overall service).

Outsourcing contracts might contain financial penalties and/or termination options if the supplier fails to meet the service levels sufficiently well. Some outsourcing contracts also contain bonuses if the supplier exceeds expectations.

Outsourcing contract negotiations can be complex and protracted, so there is always a danger that the real purpose of the negotiation gets lost in the haggling. Don't let that happen to you. The key thing to remember is that the contractual arrangements should be a fair allocation of risks and rewards between the two parties to ensure the maximum chance of success for both.

Summary

- Almost every organisation outsources some IT functions.
- Ask yourself questions about your organisation's capabilities and the acceptability of outsourcing to decide your potential scope of IT outsourcing.
- Outsourcing IT is a project much like any other, but make sure you take the TUPE employment regulations into account.
- Remember that you cannot outsource ultimate management responsibility, so don't even try it.
- Make sure that you have appropriate and measurable service level agreements to support the contract.

Technophobia and technoscepticism

CHAPTER OBJECTIVES

In this chapter we shall:

- Explain the difference between fear (technophobia) and loathing (technoscepticism) of IT.
- Help you to accept that some technophobia and technoscepticism is probably beneficial.
- Suggest some ways to avoid or at least minimise the potentially harmful effects of fear and loathing in its more extreme forms.

Fear and loathing of IT

There are two main terms for 'fear and loathing' in the IT field:

- *Technophobia:* in its milder form this is an apprehension of new technologies (e.g. new machines and programs); in its extreme form it is a fear of all technology.
- *Technoscepticism:* in its milder form this is a belief that a particular technology might not necessarily be good for you; in its extreme form it is an opposition to all technology.

Technophobia and technoscepticism have been around at least as long as the automated looms of the early 19th century (when, for example, Monsieur Jacquard of Jacquard loom fame was run out of town by angry villagers and Ned Ludd of 'luddite' fame instigated similar riots in Britain). In those cases, as often today, the fear and loathing stemmed mainly from fear of unemployment.

It is worth noting that history suggests that technology leads to more jobs, not fewer. The jobs do often change, but they usually tend to change for the better. When your staff's jobs are not at risk from an IT project, it is often a good idea to say so up front to allay fears. When some jobs are at risk, it is still a good idea to allay fears by being straightforward. If you have any sense you will provide retraining when it is needed. Again it makes sense to discuss these issues at an early stage.

Sometimes, of course, some specific jobs will be at risk as a result of an IT project – this will require sensitive and sensible handling in much the same way as any other form of job change.

Healthy fear and loathing

Even the most IT literate of us can feel some apprehension when first starting with a new computer, device or software program. Indeed, it is probably rational to feel such apprehension as it is at the 'brand new' stage that machines and programs are most likely not to work. We suggest that organisations should try to minimise pioneering risks by actively avoiding the use of leading edge devices and/or bespoke software wherever possible. In this way, you are probably only going to tread reasonably 'well-ploughed furrows' in your use of IT. That doesn't stop things from going wrong, but if your IT project is well planned you should not

---

CASE EXAMPLE   Big gun versus new kid on the block

One recent pertinent example occurred during a selection meeting for a clinical trials system for a large medical research charity. The choice seemed stark. There was the 'all-singing, all-dancing' solution from a well-known and long-established software house specialising in the clinical trials field, 'big gun'. Alternatively, there was the tidy looking but scaled down solution from a 'new kid on the block' with only a handful of references but a price tag around 20 to 25 per cent of the 'big gun's' quote. Truly there was no easy answer in this selection and the discussions were many and varied.

As high noon approached, the discussions started to hinge on the functionality provided, with advocates of the 'big gun' pointing out fancy features lacking in the 'new kid on the block's' offering. Detractors pointed out that some of those fancy features were not even in the specification we had drawn up, and the missing features which were in the specification were mostly wants more than needs.

Eventually, the Director of the group, a self-confessed technosceptic who had been silent throughout the debate so far asked one brief question. 'How many of you use more than two settings on your domestic washing machines?' No hands. 'Do you really think you would use all those extra features in 'big gun's' system?'

'New kid on the block' won the day. It was almost certainly the right choice for that organisation.

come across insurmountable problems, only interesting challenges along the way.

If you are one of the (small minority) of people who is genuinely fearful of technology, the only options open are to avoid all use of IT (not recommended) or to confront your fears by embracing IT (recommended). Many people find the best way to overcome the fear and embrace IT is to use a computer at home for non-work activities at first. The fast expansion of the internet through the world wide web makes IT a medium almost everyone can use for some aspects of their personal interests.

We believe that mild technoscepticism is healthy because many IT projects fail due to inappropriate and overly elaborate use of technology. At the planning stage, we actively encourage organisations to consider some sceptical questions, such as 'could we get 80 per cent of the benefits we seek for 20 per cent of the cost?'. Many not-for-profits have saved a great deal of money by challenging their own proposals in this way.

Avoiding the worst side effects of fear and loathing

We believe that communication while seeking contribution, consensus and commitment (see chapter 16) is beneficial to any IT project and advocate that charities should ensure that nervous and sceptical voices are actively included in such a process.

Try to help people who are openly nervous or worried about proposed changes by providing them with information and informal training/learning opportunities early on in the process. Encourage people to be open about their worries and concerns and try to address those issues during the planning stage, so those people can see that these matters are being taken into account.

It might not be possible to win round the most ardently sceptical people, but their criticisms will probably help you to improve the quality of your IT projects by thinking through their objections.

Summary

- Some fear (technophobia) and loathing (technoscepticism) can be beneficial to IT projects.
- Try to minimise the unpleasant side effects of fear and loathing through allowing open and honest expression of concerns from an early stage of IT projects.
- Help people to overcome fear arising from the unknown by finding informal ways for them to learn about IT, such as using the world wide web.

Part 5

Shared values: the internet and related technologies

Shared values: the internet and related technologies – using this part

This part covers the application of the internet and technologies arising from it to the not-for-profit sector. It consists mostly of pragmatic help with some background and reflective advice. We have included a number of web addresses, where appropriate, and apologise in advance for the fact that some of those sources are bound to change or disappear before you read this sentence. We have tried to focus mostly on directory sources, which should reduce the number of obsolete addresses in our text. If you end up really stuck, please contact the authors through www.zyen.com and we'll redirect you to a suitable source.

The initial chapter sketches the history of the internet, outlines its applicability for the not-for-profit sector and explains the basics of getting started. Most readers should read 'Intranets and extranets' for further ideas that can benefit all but the very smallest not-for-profit organisations. 'Netiquette – the dos and don'ts of sharing' is relevant to any reader who uses the internet significantly, even if your organisation has little or no presence other than your use.

The final chapter, 'E-verything', is relevant to medium-sized and larger organisations, or indeed to any reader who wishes to explore the possibilities of internet-based activities for the not-for-profit sector.

Utilising the internet

CHAPTER OBJECTIVES

In this chapter we shall:

- Provide some background information on the development of the internet.
- Summarise the main uses of the internet for not-for-profit organisations (the final chapter, 'E-verything', goes into more detail on opportunities and possibilities.
- Outline the risks, rewards, costs and benefits you should consider when considering establishing a web site for your organisation.
- Set out the basic elements you need for internet access and web presence.
- Provide tips and guidance on getting started and changing the basics.
- Point you in the right direction for progressing beyond the basics, such as fancy sites and e-commerce.

Background

The internet is a global computer network that connects governments, companies, charities, universities and many other organisations and individuals. The underlying technical infrastructure of the internet was originally pulled together by the US Defence [sic] Agency DARPA, and its early promulgation was amongst the academic community in the late 1960s and early 1970s. The advent of the user-friendly world wide web (often referred to as just 'the web') has helped feed an extraordinary expansion of internet use. The web uses a technology known as hypertext, which enables you to link text in a document to any other computer host connected to the web. Hypertext technology was in established use for other purposes for some years before 1989, when Tim Berners Lee spotted the opportunity to use it for global connection across the internet, hence establishing the web. Al Gore's involvement in the invention of the internet is a matter of some apocryphal debate.

Pundits often like to point out that radio was available to the general public for thirty-eight years before fifty million people had adopted it and television was available for thirteen years before fifty million people tuned in. Although the internet had been used for many years beforehand, the web itself reached fifty million users within four years of general availability. Indeed, use of the internet is growing so quickly that written references to the number of users tend to look ridiculous before they are published. The numbers are safely estimated to run into hundreds of millions of people worldwide and might reach one billion before this book goes to a second (web-based?) edition.

In the commercial world, the internet is already seen as an essential business tool. Some estimate that annual turnover conducted over the internet will reach trillions of dollars within the next few years, of which:

- Tens of billions is expected to be 'retail' purchases (often referred to in the press these days as B2C – 'business to consumer').
- The rest (i.e. the vast majority) being business to business electronic trading (referred to as B2B).

What's in it for the not-for-profit sector?

There are three main aspects of the internet that should concern not-for-profit organisations:

- Electronic mail communications (distribution and receipt of information) including electronic file transfer.
- Mailing lists and discussion groups for information, collaboration and shared learning.
- The web for access to readily available information and opportunities for your organisation, as a medium for providing readily accessible information *about* your organisation, plus all the above.

Risks and rewards of setting up and maintaining a web site

When considering setting up a web site for your organisation, as with any other IT project, you should carefully consider your objectives, the scope of the project and the benefits you seek (see chapters 14 and 15). Many not-for-profit organisations seem to be 'jumping on the world wide web bandwagon', setting up web sites that are poorly thought through and not particularly beneficial.

Table 21.1, overleaf, summarises the main purposes, potential benefits and possible pitfalls for not-for-profit organisations having a web presence.

When thinking about setting up a web site, you should consider the following cost areas:

- Your charity's internet access.
- Connection to an internet service provider (ISP).
- Registration of a domain name or names (see 'Domain naming', below).
- Additional security required (e.g. electronic 'firewalls' to prevent unauthorised access to your systems).
- Web page development.
- Data linking (if needed).
- Additional hardware and software.
- Training.
- Ongoing running costs of all of the above.

Sadly, but predictably, low investment web sites are unlikely to attract many visitors other than people who would be in touch with you anyway. A recent survey by CustomerSat.com showed a direct relationship between web site budgets and traffic. Of those who invested less than $10,000 (and in the UK you can usually read £ = $ in the IT world), 60 per cent reported fewer than 100 visits per day to their site. Of those who spent between $50,000 and $100,000, 73 per cent reported more than 100 visits per day (20 per cent reported more than 1000 visits per day).

Despite the above comments on low investment web sites, it probably makes sense for most organisations to establish some form of web presence, as a positioning statement if for no other reason. This is perhaps analogous with being in the telephone directory. Your organisation might not be able to afford a large box advert, indeed you might not believe that a large advert would do you any good, but you certainly would want to be listed. The same principle applies to having some form of web presence, however minimal. Just don't expect a web presence suddenly to transform your fundraising capabilities unless your not-for-profit organisation itself has an intrinsic affinity with the web (see, for example, the Youthnet case study, in part 6).

The ongoing costs and effort involved in maintaining a decent web site can be considerable. Your site is unlikely to maintain your target audience's interest unless you keep it up to date and regularly add new items of interest. The effort involved is analogous with running a regular newsletter. The costs also have some-

TABLE 21.1 Purposes, benefits and pitfalls of web sites

Purposes	Potential benefits	Possible pitfalls
Communicating information about your charity	■ Campaigning and/or advocacy ■ Attracting membership and/or support ■ Providing information to beneficiaries, stakeholders and other interested parties ■ Demonstrating your knowledge and eminence in a given field ■ A 'shop window' from which supporters might volunteer, request additional information etc.	■ If you do not keep the web site up to date, your site might have an adverse rather than a positive effect
Fundraising	■ Collecting donations, covenants, sponsorships etc. ■ Running on-line games, lotteries etc. to raise funds ■ An additional medium for trading (e.g. Christmas cards, mail order goods)	■ At the time of writing, there is little evidence to suggest that the web is able to generate revenues to cover the costs of setting up a web presence for fundraising purposes alone (this might change during the life of this book) ■ You need to take care over regulatory, legal and tax implications of gaming and trading on the web
Procurement	■ Increasing the economy and efficiency of procurement (through electronic data interchange or electronic commerce – 'e-trading') ■ Benefiting from economies of scale if done through a shared subscription e.g. with other charities	■ You possibly need little or no web presence of your own to achieve the benefits, so you should not necessarily cost justify your web project based on electronic procurement
Direct provision of your services	■ Would vary from charity to charity ■ In the case of advocacy and campaigning organisations, some of the benefits set out in 'Communicating information about your charity', above, would constitute direct provision ■ Probably the most compelling argument for a significant web presence at present, for those charities for whom it is appropriate	■ Can you reach an appropriate audience through the web? ■ You need to be careful not to exclude some potential supporters and/or beneficiaries – therefore the web is likely to be an 'as well as' service rather than an 'instead of' service

thing in common with a newsletter; the higher the quality of production you seek, the more your site is likely to cost. However, if you do not want or need 'bells and whistles' the ongoing costs can be very low.

The key messages are: think before you jump into the web and make sure that when you do, you do so as a medium to long-term investment based on defined objectives and measurable benefits. And if you can't afford a giant leap, try a small step.

Internet basics

Gaining access to the internet (without establishing a presence of your own) is a pretty straightforward and low cost affair these days. Most readers will have been bombarded with free trial offers for internet access through newspapers, magazines and direct mail. If you have not tried it before, there is a great deal to be said for using these free trials as a way of learning and having a go. You will pay for telephone calls (normally at a local rate) but if you have 'free access' (i.e. pay no monthly subscription) there will be no other cost. If nothing else, you can visit the research and resource web sites highlighted in this chapter. If you are at a loss to know where to start researching other areas of interest, use search engine sites to help you; www.altavista.com, www.askjeeves.com and www.dogpile.com are some of the authors' favourites.

Most readers of this chapter presumably wish to have or rethink some form of web presence as well as access to the internet. Once you have decided the purposes and benefits you are seeking from your web presence (see table 21.1) and your intended audiences (e.g. volunteers, supporters, beneficiaries, trade customers) you can make some decisions about the site's presentation and content.

The process of thinking through presentation and content is analogous to publishing in other media. It usually makes sense for the person responsible for external communications and publishing to take responsibility. Key factors to bear in mind include:

- What do you want your web site address to be?
- To what extent do you intend to promote your site?
- Do you intend to do your own web design or employ someone to do it?
- Do you intend to sell goods over the site?
- Will you accept advertising on the site from software and service providers connected with the site? (often a good way to keep down costs).
- Will you sell advertising on your site? (even some small not-for-profit organisations have valuable name recognition which can make this a viable proposition).

Internet service provision and web site hosting

Unless you are quite a large organisation, you will almost certainly want to use another party to host your web site. internet service providers (ISPs) usually offer some form of hosting service, but do make sure you check that the ISP is offering the type of services you want at a price you can afford. You do not have to use your ISP for web hosting, of course, although it can make your life easier to use a single supplier for your internet access and web hosting.

Whoever you use, make sure you understand what you can and cannot do on your web space. Some low price and free services forbid trading through their space, for example. Others charge through the nose as soon as you want services outside the scope of the free or low cost service. However, not-for-profit organisations with modest ambitions can usually get started for little or no outlay for web space. At the time of writing there are many free hosting services (not just targeted at the not-for-profit sector), but those available to you might not offer the services you want and might insist on prominent advertising for themselves. Look at Geocities (www.geocities.yahoo.com), Megspace (www.megspace.com) and several aimed specifically at the not-for profit sector (find through www.itforcharities.co.uk).

Changing ISP is not a difficult or traumatic affair when switching internet access. If you have been using a low cost / free 'home use style' service (such as Tesco or Freeserve) for access only and find that they are unable to offer you the services you now want at a price you can afford, your new ISP should be able to get you up and running quickly and easily. It can be a little more tricky if you have an existing web site and wish to change hosting (see below).

Domain naming

Many hosting organisations will provide you with a site name linked to their domain, possibly free, but the site name can be a bit of a mouthful, such as www.ourcharity.whatabargainwebhost.com. If you want your own domain name, enabling you to have a site name such as www.ourcharity.org, you will need to register your own domain name. It's often cheaper to register your domain name through your ISP than it is to do it yourself. It can cost you anything from £50 to £250 as many ISPs bundle the costs into their service price, so you are effectively paying over time for the service. The costs increase if you are keen to protect your name by using multiple registrations (e.g. ourcharity.org, ourcharity.co.uk, ourcharity.net and ourcharity.com).

If someone has already used your name, you might need to use your imagination a bit to choose a suitable domain name. At the time of writing, all three letter combinations in conjunction with .com had already been snapped up and the four letter combinations were going fast! You might be able to regain use of your domain name if your organisation's name is a registered trademark and if you can afford the time and cost of a fight. To be honest, as long as the site name is reasonably short and clearly identifies your organisation, that should be sufficient for most not-for-profit uses.

Design

The next step to think about is the design. Simple sites are very easy to produce. Web browsers such as Microsoft's internet Explorer and Netscape Communicator come with free web page editors that work fine for simple web pages. It is possible to get more sophisticated free or cheap web design software through the internet. Look out for the phrases 'freeware' and 'shareware'. Freeware is software that the author has issued genuinely free of charge (often to get you used to it and then entice you to buy the more sophisticated versions of the same software, sometimes due to pure altruism), for example CSE Validator (www.htmlvalidator.com). Shareware is software which you can try free of charge but for which you are honour bound to pay (usually a modest fee, say £10 to £100) if you want to continue using it. Consider CoffeeCup www.coffeecup.com and HotDog www.sausage.com as two possible shareware choices.

Commercial and straightforward web design products include Microsoft FrontPage and Macromedia Dreamweaver. Expect to pay between £100 and £400 if you go along this road. The expenditure might well be worth it, however, especially if a fully functional and well documented product is going to save you time and/or web design fees.

Whichever web design product you use, you will probably want to add graphic images or resources. Check out webMonkey, http://hotwired.lycos.com/webmonkey and eFuse www.efuse.com (to name but two) for information, sources and ideas.

Alternatively, you might wish to use a web design company. There are thousands to choose from and the web sites mentioned above will provide you with more choice than you could possibly handle. The web site www.itforcharities.co.uk lists many companies with not-for-profit sector experience, which might or might not be a good idea for you. The initial cost might well be modest (say £200 to £400) but do bear in mind that you might end up having to pay the designer to maintain the site for you if you do not cultivate those skills in-house. That might cost £40 to £60 an hour, which can add up to a significant amount every time you want to add new events, causes, press releases, product details or volunteering information. There really is little point in putting up a web site unless you are committed to keeping it up to date and maintaining it.

Changing the basics

Once your organisation is up and running, you might want to change your set up. For a start, you might have chosen an ISP and/or web host whose service seems erratic or whose services and/or price structures suddenly change in a way you don't like. Or perhaps you have recently joined a not-for-profit organisation only to find that the internet access and web presence are not to your liking but nobody quite knows who set it up or how it works. We come across this problem regularly in smaller and medium-sized not-for-profits, especially where some or all of the services were provided as gifts in kind. The checklist opposite sets out the basic questions you should ask and get answered in order to investigate and assess your web presence provision.

CASE EXAMPLE   The Actors' Workshop web site

This small charity works with young people in the Calderdale community, introducing them to drama as an alternative to trauma or troublemaking. Run full-time by one technophobe (Mike Ward) and a large hoard of enthusiastic young people, there is hardly any money. In-house skills are directed towards performing arts rather than web design (see also the case example in the Introduction).

Mike was approached by a small local web design company, Fizzbomb Design, who offered to design a web site for the workshop, have the site hosted by Calderdale.net and maintain the site, all in return for prominent advertising and publicity.

Check out the site at www.actorsworkshop. org.uk. The site is simple but effective. A site of this kind is within the means of most not-for-profit organisations, even if the organisation has to pay for the resources used to design and maintain it.

One of the more effective features of this site is the reviews section, where visitors can write and/or read reviews of shows. This is an excellent way of getting the Actors' Workshop supporters to help keep content vibrant and topical. See if you can spot the self-serving review by one of this book's authors! Your not-for-profit organisation might have similar or analogous ideas which will help maintain interest in your site.

ASSESSING ISP AND WEB HOSTING PROVISION CHECKLIST

ISP and web site hosting

- ☑ Who is your ISP?
- ☑ Who is hosting your web site?
- ☑ To what extent was web site hosting linked to the domain name registration?
- ☑ What period does the current hosting contract cover?
- ☑ What is the disk capacity of the current subscription?
- ☑ What was the cost of the current subscription?
- ☑ Did your organisation bear some or all of this cost?
- ☑ Is it anticipated that your organisation will bear this cost in future?
- ☑ Are there any significant limits to disk capacity available through this host?

Domain name registration

- ☑ Do you have your own domain name(s) or is/are your domain name(s) linked to your host?
- ☑ Who registered the domain name(s)?
- ☑ With/through whom were they registered?
- ☑ Precisely what names have been registered?
- ☑ For what period do the registrations apply?
- ☑ What is the mechanism for maintaining registrations?
- ☑ What has been paid for registrations?
- ☑ Did your organisation bear this cost?
- ☑ What is the anticipated cost of maintaining registrations?
- ☑ Is it anticipated that your organisation will bear this cost in future?

Web site design and maintenance

- ☑ Who designed the current web site?
- ☑ Who is maintaining it?
- ☑ To what extent is web site maintenance linked to web site hosting?
- ☑ What has been paid for such services to date?
- ☑ Did your organisation bear some or all of this cost?
- ☑ Is it anticipated that your organisation will bear this cost in future?
- ☑ What software tools are in use for your organisation's web site?
- ☑ Are these tools readily available for standard PCs such as those in use at your organisation?
- ☑ If yes, what do such tools cost?

☑ If the tools are not readily available or are prohibitively expensive,
   what would it take to convert your site into a tool set that is readily
   available at low or no cost to your organisation?

Changing your web site host needs some planning and thought.
For a start, if you do not have your own domain name, you will
have to change web site address. You can redirect from your old
address to your new one, but this usually involves some cost. The
thought process and issues are analogous with changing telephone number. Your new web host ought to be able to solve these
issues with you. Even if you have your own domain name and a
good new host, it can take an inordinate amount of time (and
effort on the host's part) to get your domain switched over to the
new host. This is 'not really your problem' if you have agreed a
scope of work and fees, but we urge caution against promising
your trustees 'we shall be off that service by such-and-such a date'.

Beyond the basics

Whole books are being written on the fancy things you can do
using internet technologies, so we feel daunted trying to go too
far beyond the basics in this practical tips chapter. Chapter 24
explores the ideas that many of you should be thinking about in
the immediate or near future.

Beyond the basics of internet access, if you have several people
in your office regularly accessing the internet, you should consider installing a dedicated line to an ISP to reduce telephone
charge costs and probably improve speed of access. You can get
started for as little as £400 to £600 installation cost and £3500 to
£5000 per annum. This might seem like a lot of money until you
work out how much you might spend on telephone calls. If you
are a larger organisation with several people using the internet at
any one time, you are likely to want higher capacity so the costs
shown above might double. If you really are in the internet-based
information provision business, the costs might be even higher.
Very often, the increase in your internet use coincides with an
increase in your organisation's activity through its web presence,
so it is often a good time to review the whole of your internet
access and web hosting service provider(s).

As your site progresses, you will probably want it to become
increasingly interactive. If you are looking after your own site,
you will then need to pick up some tools and skills beyond those
discussed in 'Design', above. For example, common gateway
interface (CGI) scripts can be used to:

- Add security to your site (e.g. to have a section of your site available only to registered volunteers).
- Process forms (e.g. grant application forms).
- Personalise content (e.g. showing supporters only those web pages that reflect their declared interests).

Sites that will help you to learn about making your web site more dynamic include www.cgi101.com, www.web-authoring.com and www.beseen.com.

If you want to take donations over the web, you will need to get internet merchant status from your bank (this can be painful) or use the services of a payment service provider (PSP). There are several PSPs available at a price, including www.worldpay.com and www.secpay.com. Several with not-for-profit sector experience are listed on www.itforcharities.co.uk.

If you want to move more down the road of electronic trading, do look before you leap. You will need to invest considerable time and effort to get set up for full-blown electronic trading and there are very few not-for-profit organisations that are likely to generate sufficient trading revenues to justify the costs. Chapter 24 discusses these aspects in more detail.

Summary

- The internet has emerged in the past few years, becoming a medium that not-for-profit organisations can no longer ignore.
- As with all projects, consider your objectives, the scope of the project and the benefits you seek; don't just jump on the bandwagon without thinking.
- Make sure you understand the risks, rewards, costs and benefits of your choices. In particular, don't expect a web presence to transform your fundraising capabilities, and do take into account the costs and effort involved in keeping your web site up to date and interesting.
- Don't ponder too much – if in doubt, do something cheap and simple and take it from there.
- It is not difficult or expensive to establish a basic internet presence, especially if your initial ambitions are quite modest – resources available on the internet itself will help you to get started.
- Choose an internet service provider (ISP) and web host capable of meeting your immediate and foreseeable needs, making sure you understand what it is likely to cost. Don't change suppliers for trivial reasons, but don't be afraid to change.
- Either design your own site (perfectly feasible for many) or use a third party at modest cost for a basic site; most importantly

remember that you will need procedures, time and/or budgets for keeping the site up to date.

- Explore going beyond the basics, especially into areas that link with your not-for-profit's specific activities.

Intranets and extranets

CHAPTER OBJECTIVES

In this chapter we shall:

- Explain what intranets and extranets are.
- Set out some thoughts on how they can be useful for not-for-profit organisations.
- Assess the risks and rewards of using intranets and extranets in not-for-profit organisations.

What are intranets?

An intranet is basically an in-house web site: you utilise the same software and technology that you might be using for your world wide web presence to build an 'organisation wide web' for internal purposes. The result should be easy to use, relatively inexpensive and should help you to keep your web site up to date. In the 1999 survey *Information and Communication Technologies: Reshaping the Voluntary Sector*, (Burt and Taylor, 1999) about 25 per cent of not-for-profit organisations claimed to be using intranet technologies and a further 21 per cent expected to be doing so within a few years. Adoption of intranets does not seem to depend on size; both large and small not-for-profit organisations seem to be taking it up. This is probably because the need for additional technology is negligible if you already have the capability for web presence and use.

Figure 22.1 illustrates what intranets are and where they fit in to your organisational networks and the world wide web.

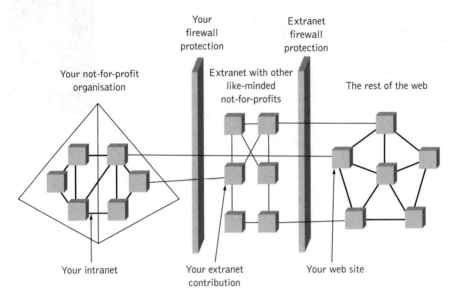

FIGURE 22.1 Intranets, extranets and the web

Using intranets

Possible intranet uses for not-for-profit organisations include:

- *Internal communications* – discussion groups, group calendar, document management, news.
- *Human resources* – staff handbook, directory and surveys, internal recruitment.
- *Fundraising* – scripts and training, forecasts and reports, lead management.
- *IT* – user documentation, software circulation, IT training.
- *Finance* – report circulation, budgeting, expense claims, requisitioning, time sheets.

Potential rewards and benefits

- Reduction in the use of paper – this benefit has been promised many times before and not delivered, but the message from the corporate sector is that the adoption of intranets does cut down on internal paper.
- Connectivity – you can use your intranet to connect users of devices that you have previously found hard to connect (e.g. PCs with Macs with old terminal devices) and to connect users from remote sites (e.g. through the modem links and web browsers they might already be using for web access).

- Ease of use – if you can 'surf the web' you can surf your organisation's intranet.
- Keeping in-house information up to date – this might be more easily achieved on-line than it was on paper, but it does still have to be done.
- Keeping information provision to third parties up to date – your intranet can be, in effect, a superset of your web presence (i.e. part of your intranet is available in the public domain, part is retained privately within your network). You are therefore able to keep your web presence up to date by maintaining your intranet.
- Building a learning culture – providing an environment for collaboration, information exchange and sharing knowledge.

Potential risks or pitfalls

- 'Scope creep' – intranet projects run the risk of being unstructured and therefore never ending (if, indeed, you can ever agree on a basis to get started).
- 'Cost creep' – especially pertinent if you are a victim of scope creep and you are using a third party for the management of design and content.
- Dashed expectations and hopes – many not-for-profit organisations enter intranet projects with the best of intentions, but promise more than their staff and/or wallet can deliver.
- Publishing conflict – lack of clarity about who owns the content, who can put items up, what should be public and what should be private.
- Security lapse – organisations need to have sufficient IT security in place, especially if your intranet is a superset of your web presence (see 'Potential rewards and benefits', above). You need to use 'firewall' technology (such as secure routers and firewall software – see Shields Up! at www.gr.com) appropriately to protect your private information.

What are extranets?

Figure 22.1 illustrates what extranets are and shows where they fit in to your organisational networks and the world wide web.

An extranet is basically a club of organisations which privately connect, probably using the internet as the networking medium. As with intranets, you mainly utilise the same software and technology that you might use for your web presence to share information and/or operations, e.g. with suppliers, donors, members, volunteers, other not-for-profit organisations. In *Information and Communication Technologies: Reshaping the Voluntary Sector* (op. cit.), about 2 per cent of not-for-profit organisations claimed to be using extranet technologies. Whereas intranets would often benefit from, but do not require additional use of technology, extranets often require additional use of technologies such as:

- XML (eXtensible Markup Language, an extended form of hypertext which enables web pages to function like database records).
- Java (a web-friendly programming language).
- Password security, database extensions, common gateway interface (CGI – see previous chapter) interactivity.
- Other add-ons which go 'whoosh' and 'ping' to enable you to show off to your peers.

Using extranets

Extranet uses for not-for-profit organisations include:

- *'Club' communications* – discussion groups, document exchange, news, 'club' diary.
- *Members and volunteers* – training and support, group information exchange, 'clubs within clubs'.
- *E-commerce* – consortium procurement, club trading, e-banking, awards management.
- *Campaigning and advocacy* – liaising with intermediaries, interface with influencers and peers.
- *Grant making* – applications management, refereeing, peer review and consultation.

Potential rewards and benefits

- Operational time saved – mostly from encouraging constituents (e.g. members, volunteers, grant holders) to choose 'self-service' and other efficient work methods.
- Effort and cost savings through e-procurement – both efficiencies in processing and economies of scale arising through 'clubbing' (such as forming procurement consortia or providing a shared service with other like-minded not-for-profits).
- Improved effectiveness in comparatively intangible areas of your work, such as advocacy and community liaison.

Potential risks or pitfalls

- Agreeing scope – any reader who has ever tried to get a not-for-profit consortium of any kind moving will recognise the difficulties in finding and agreeing common ground (there is a high risk of never agreeing on a basis to get started).

- Cost sharing – you need to find ways of fairly sharing the costs of a collaborative development and its ongoing maintenance.
- Harmonising expectations – it's hard enough to manage realistic expectations within one organisation, but in this instance you need to manage those expectations across several. Further, different organisations might have very different goals from the initiative.
- Security – each participating organisation needs to take responsibility for its own IT security, but the 'club' needs to set procedures and minimum standards to ensure the integrity of the 'clubbed' information.

Summary

- Intranets and extranets enable you to extend the use of internet technologies to benefit your own organisation and/or your not-for-profit 'community'.
- Intranets have the potential for relatively high rewards for a relatively low investment in cost, effort and risk management (but do manage those risks).
- Extranets have the potential for high rewards but tend to require a little more technology and a greater investment in collaboration.
- Agreeing the scope of initiatives and managing expectations are once again key factors in ensuring success with intranets and extranets.

Netiquette – the dos and don'ts of sharing

CHAPTER OBJECTIVES

In this chapter we shall:

■ Set out some guidelines on the etiquette of e-mail and the use of shared networks.
■ Provide tips on how these guidelines might be applied sensibly to your organisation.
■ Encourage you to be 'good net citizens' by setting out the appropriate ten commandments.

Netiquette sources

There is a plethora of guides available on 'netiquette' – the etiquette of e-mail and use of the shared networks (e.g. your organisation's network, intranet, extranet and/or the internet). The following set of tips borrows (legitimately) from two of the most useful public domain sources at the time of writing:

■ *Netiquette Guidelines: Responsible use of the Network Working Group's* RFC1855 (Hambridge, 1995)
■ *The Net: User Guidelines and Netiquette* (Rinaldi, 1998)

Netiquette tips and the ten commandments

Listed below are generic netiquette tips and some useful comments specifically for not-for-profit organisations. These tips apply both to the use of internet network facilities and to private network facilities (e.g. your organisation's network, intranet or an extranet) and so you can use them as a basis for your own guidelines or policies on the use of such facilities.

Electronic mail (e-mail) box

The content and maintenance of a user's electronic mailbox is the user's responsibility:

- Check e-mail daily and remain within your disk space quota.
- Delete unwanted messages immediately as they take up disk storage.
- Keep messages remaining in your electronic mailbox to a minimum.
- Download mail messages or extract them to files then to disks for future reference.
- Unless you are using a powerful encryption device you should assume that others may be able to read or access your mail.

In a not-for-profit organisation, it is often sensible to retain your mail messages, but this is usually best achieved by saving messages to a secure, private work area.

Public disk storage area

The content and maintenance of a user's disk storage area is the user's responsibility:

- Keep files to a minimum – files should be downloaded to your personal computer's hard drive or to diskettes.
- Routinely and frequently virus-scan your system, especially when receiving or downloading files from other systems.
- Your files may be accessible by people with system privileges, so do not maintain anything private in your disk storage area.

Not-for-profit organisations with local networks should have policies regarding storing files – it is often sensible to require staff to store all their data files on a local network drive rather than their PC's drive.

Anonymous File Transfer Protocol (FTP)

FTP is a means by which users deposit and collect files using the internet as the medium for transfer:

- Users should respond to the PASSWORD prompt with their e-mail address, so if that site chooses, it can track the level of FTP usage.
- When possible limit downloads, especially large downloads (1Mb+), to after normal business hours locally and, for the remote FTP host, preferably late in the evening.

- Adhere to time restrictions as requested by archive sites. Think in terms of the current time at the site that's being visited, not of local time.
- Copy downloaded files to your personal computer hard drive or disks to remain within your disk quota.
- Do not use someone else's FTP site to deposit materials you wish other people to pick up. This is called 'dumping' and is not generally acceptable behaviour.
- It's the user's responsibility when downloading programs to check for copyright or licensing agreements. If the program is beneficial to your use, pay any author's registration fee. If there is any doubt, don't copy it – there have been many occasions on which copyrighted software has found its way into FTP archives. Support for any downloaded programs should be requested from the originator of the application. Remove unwanted programs from your systems.

Be vigilant with regard to software viruses when downloading files using FTP or equivalent, even when the source is well known to you.

E-mail security, brevity and identification

- Do not give your user ID or password to another person. System administrators who need to access your account for maintenance or to correct problems will have full privileges to your account.
- Do not assume your e-mail messages are private nor that they can be read by only yourself or the recipient.
- Keep paragraphs and messages short and to the point – more than fifty lines is normally considered long.
- Try to be brief without being overly terse.
- Limit line length to approximately sixty-five to seventy characters and avoid control characters.
- Do not send chain letters through the internet. Sending them can cause the loss of your internet access, through your ISP withdrawing services from you, or other ISPs refusing to service material routed by your lax ISP.
- When quoting another person, edit out whatever isn't directly applicable to your reply. Take the time to edit any quotations down to the minimum necessary to provide context for your reply.
- Focus on one subject per message and always include a pertinent subject title for the message, that way the user can locate the message quickly.
- Include your signature at the bottom of e-mail messages when communicating with people who may not know you personally or when broadcasting to a changing group of subscribers.

- Your signature footer is in effect your electronic business card – it should include your name, position, affiliation and internet address and should not exceed four lines. Optional information could include your address and phone number and activation of an e-business card.

These principles apply as much to intra and inter organisation e-mail as they do to the wider internet.

Not-for-profit organisations should have a policy regarding the use of the organisation's e-mail system for private correspondence. They should also have a policy regarding the authorisation of expenditure and/or opinions expressed in e-mails in much the same way as you should have such a policy for other types of correspondence.

E-mail manners and form

- Capitalise words only to highlight an important point or to distinguish a title or heading. Capitalising whole words that are not titles is generally termed as SHOUTING!
- *Asterisks* surrounding a word can be used to make a stronger point.
- Avoid misinterpretation of dates by including the spelled out month: e.g. 24 June 2001 or June 24 2001.
- Follow chain of command procedures for corresponding with superiors. For example, don't send a complaint via e-mail directly to the 'top' just because you can.
- Be professional and careful what you say about others; e-mail is easily forwarded.
- Wait overnight before sending emotional responses to messages.
- Cite all quotes, references and sources and respect copyright and license agreements.
- It is considered extremely rude to forward personal e-mail to mailing lists or Usenet without the original author's permission.
- If you think the importance of the e-mail justifies it, immediately reply to let the sender know you received it, even if you will send a longer reply later.
- Bear in mind that the cost of sending an e-mail message is, on average, shared equally between the sender and the recipient.
- Be careful when using sarcasm and humour. Without face to face communications your joke may be viewed as criticism. When being humorous, use emoticons to express humour (tilt your head to the left to see the emoticon smile) :-) = happy face for humour.
- Acronyms can be used to abbreviate when possible; however, messages that are filled with acronyms can be confusing and annoying to the reader.

Examples: IMHO= in my humble/honest opinion
FYI = for your information
BTW = by the way

These principles apply as much to intra and inter organisation e-mail as they do to the wider internet.

Staff in not-for-profit organisations should be especially careful to avoid inadvertently offending potential readers' sensibilities.

Mailing lists and discussion groups

- Some mailing lists have low rates of traffic, others can flood your mailbox with several hundred mail messages per day. Numerous incoming messages from various listservers or mailing lists by multiple users require extensive system processing which can tie up valuable resources. Subscription to interest groups or discussion lists should be kept to a minimum and should not exceed what your disk quota – or you – can handle.
- When you join a list, monitor the messages for a few days to get a feel for what common questions are asked, and what topics are deemed off-limits. This is commonly referred to as 'lurking'. When you feel comfortable with the group, then start posting.
- See if there is a FAQ (frequently asked questions) area for a group that you are interested in joining. Veteran members get annoyed when they see the same questions every few weeks.
- Follow any and all guidelines that the listowner has posted; she/he establishes the local 'netiquette' standards for her/his list.
- Keep your questions and comments relevant to the focus of the discussion group (even if others seem to be breaking this rule).

Not-for-profit organisations should have a policy on access to and use of discussion groups – especially with regard to membership of groups not directly related to your work.

There are Usenet and world wide web discussion groups covering many areas of interest to not-for-profit organisations, both in general and in specialised not-for-profit sector fields. See the Directory (in Appendix B) for links to not-for-profit oriented discussion groups and other relevant forums.

World wide web

- Do not assume that information you find is up to date and/or accurate. Remember that new technology has allowed just about anyone to be a publisher, but not everyone has discovered the responsibilities that accompany publishing.
- Do not include very large graphic images in your html documents. It is preferable to have postage sized images that the

user can click on to 'enlarge' a picture. Some users with access to the web are viewing documents using slow modems, and downloading images can take some time.

- It is not a requirement to ask permission to link to someone else's site, but out of respect for the individual and their efforts, a simple e-mail message stating that you have made a link would be appropriate – you might also politely request that they link their site back to yours to return the favour.
- When including video or voice files, include next to the description a file size, i.e. (10Kb or 2Mb), so the user has the option of knowing how long it will take to download the file.
- Keep naming standards for URLs simple and not overly excessive with changes in case. Some users do not realise that sites are case sensitive or they receive URLs verbally where case sensitivity is not easily recognisable.
- When in doubt about a URL, try accessing the domain address first, then navigate through the site to locate the specific URL. Most URLs begin with the node address of www followed by the site address, e.g. www.cren.ch, www.fau.edu, www.ibm.com, www.cpsr.org.
- A URL that includes only an image map and no text might not be accessible to those users that do not have access to a graphical web browser (such as Internet Explorer or Netscape). Always include the option of text links in your URL documents.
- World wide web connections can be very high bandwidth customers. With graphical web browsers, when graphic images are not necessary to obtain information, it is a good idea, both in terms of the speed of the session and to conserve bandwidth, to set the options to 'turn off' or 'delay' inline images.
- URL authors should always protect their additions to the web by including trademark (TM) or copyright (©) symbols in their html documents.
- URL authors should include an e-mail address at the bottom (or in the address area) of all html documents. Because of the nature of html links, a user can automatically link to your html document and have questions about it, but will not know who to contact if the e-mail address is not available.
- Including the actual URL in the document source, preferably after the <Address> tag, will allow users who print out the information to know where to access the information in the future, e.g. URL – *http://www.fau.edu/netiquette/web.html*.
- URL authors should always include the date the site was last updated – so users linking to the site can know how up to date the information is.
- Infringement of copyright laws, obscene, harassing or threatening materials on web sites can be in violation of local, state,

national or international laws and can be subject to litigation by the appropriate law enforcement agency. Authors of html documents will ultimately be responsible for what they allow users worldwide to access.

It is especially important for not-for-profit organisations to tailor their web presence to enable those with low specification equipment to access information effectively – minimise exclusion by maximising simplicity.

Not-for-profit organisations should have policies with regard to publishing documents on the world wide web – these policies can mirror your policies with regard to publishing generally – the world wide web is simply another medium – albeit a far reaching one.

The ten commandments for computer ethics (from the Computer Ethics Institute)

1   Thou shalt not use a computer to harm other people.
2   Thou shalt not interfere with other people's computer work.
3   Thou shalt not snoop around in other people's files.
4   Thou shalt not use a computer to steal.
5   Thou shalt not use a computer to bear false witness.
6   Thou shalt not use or copy software for which you have not paid.
7   Thou shalt not use other people's computer resources without authorisation.
8   Thou shalt not appropriate other people's intellectual output.
9   Thou shalt think about the social consequences of the program you write.
10 Thou shalt use a computer in ways that show consideration and respect.

Not-for-profit organisations should be vigilant to ensure that they are not breaking these 'commandments'. Number 6 seems to be the one that many not-for-profit organisations struggle to keep, even though they can often get low price (or in some cases legitimately free) licences for much software.

Summary

- Following the netiquette rules and the ten commandments should improve your ability to benefit from using networks and help you to help others to benefit.

- Most of the rules are common sense, but the sort of common sense that it is aided by an occasional read and using the rules and commandments as reference material.
- You can use the material in this chapter as the basis of your organisation's policies for network use, embracing your organisational network, intranets, extranets and the internet.

E-verything

CHAPTER OBJECTIVES

In this chapter we shall:

- Consider the media and business worlds' preoccupation with inter-connecting technologies prefixed with the letter 'e'.
- Discuss the implications of this changing world for not-for-profit organisations of all shapes and sizes.
- Try to open your minds to the possibilities for your organisation.

Examples of web sites are scattered throughout this chapter. Companies and their web sites change rapidly. These examples are not recommendations and interested readers should use the web addresses as a starting point for their online research.

E-xpectation

Information technology has been rising in popularity – it's the 'very thing' these days. The marked rise in the popularity of everything to do with the internet has accompanied a rise in software, hardware and other related technologies' trendiness. Technology is more understandable and more personal than ever before. Journalists are using technology for their daily work and are writing about the businesses that make the technology they use. These businesses are 'good copy': fortunes are made; fortunes are lost. Floods of advertising accompanies each business launch, further increasing the interest in technology. People are discussing technology around water coolers, at dinner parties and in the pub. It seems that everything to do with inter-connecting technologies is being pre-fixed with 'e'. There is a sense of expectation.

If you can imagine 'e' in everything you do, you can probably conceive of some practical, significant advances. Try and imagine e-verything your not-for-profit organisation does being inter-connected – fundraising, word processing, personnel, charitable information, stocks and legacies. Imagine e-veryone you deal with is inter-connected – donors, beneficiaries, regulators, consumers, suppliers and trustees. In some ways, this inter-connected world is frightening to people used to established ways of working. Financial analysts find that many individual shareholders already know more than they do about key companies. Civil servants find that many ordinary citizens know more than they do about planning applications, public health programmes or environmental issues. But in other ways this inter-connected world is liberating. You do not need to provide the same information repeatedly; machines can do this for you. You do not need advisors who merely provide you with access to basic sources; you can search for what you need. You can gather the information you require to effect change. You can speed up the process of change by getting the right information to the right person in the right place much closer to the right time.

However, e-verything as a thought experiment also raises valid questions. Is this inter-connected world around the corner for not-for-profit organisations? Ten years away? Twenty? Is this inter-connected world going to be too complex or too confusing? What happens to individual rights, to privacy, to legal and regulatory boundaries? What do we do if these systems break down?

Looking ahead within the foreseeable future for not-for-profit organisations, let's examine just three aspects of 'e-verything':

- E-commerce – the use of the internet and other technologies to sell what we do, to donors, beneficiaries or the wider public.
- E-procurement – the use of the internet and other technologies to purchase goods or services which we require.
- ASPs (application service providers) – the use of services delivered over the internet which help us automate our work.

E-commerce

E-commerce is using the internet to sell. There is a host of good examples – from software to books to automobiles. There is a strong distinction between the B2C (business to consumer) sale and the B2B (business to business) sale. While B2C is a reasonably large and growing market, B2B is predicted to be ten times as large and is rapidly growing.

The best way to learn about B2C e-commerce is to buy things personally over the web. A good, straightforward B2C example is one of the early leaders, www.amazon.com (or www.amazon.co.uk). For example, buy another copy of this book for a friend using e-commerce. Notice the comparatively fast load times, the search facilities, the linked recommendations, the ability to record possible future purchases, e-mail confirmations, gift tokens, category browsing, one-click buying, order tracking and even auctions. There is a host of other sites you can browse – try www.ebay.com for auctions, www.letsbuyit.com for reverse auctions, www.smartshop.com for price searching, www.schwab.com (or www.schwab-europe.com) for shares or www.expedia.com for airline tickets.

Many of the same design issues apply to B2B transactions. However, B2B is more complicated because organisations are, when you think about it, more diverse than people. There are dormant businesses, sole traders, one-site organisations, multi-office organisations, multi-national organisations, group companies, etc. Businesses have more payment mechanisms available than individuals, not just credit cards but all forms of bank payment. The early leaders in B2B sales have typically sold something that a wide range of businesses buy in a similar way, e.g. stationery. However, newer markets are proliferating at such a rate that oversupply may well be a problem. With so many ways of selling, how can you choose what to use?

Different not-for-profit organisations can use e-commerce in many different ways. A good starting point is to look at your web site from the point of view of a quick visitor. Can they easily find the information they need to make a donation or buy goods in a traditional way, e.g. over the phone or by post? Can they download some forms for post or fax? Can they send you an e-mail with some obvious fields filled in, e.g. to whom, subject, terms and conditions? Getting the basics right is often all that's needed, especially for a small not-for-profit organisation. After the easy basics are done, you can consider moving to full e-commerce. Online donation is an obvious start. Another possibility is having promotional goods online, relevant books or relevant goods for beneficiaries. Yet more possibilities include full relationship management, accounts for donors and beneficiaries, dynamically tailored and delivered information and transaction histories for everyone on what the relationship has been.

There is a big jump in e-commerce from letting people know that you have goods available and facilitating their orders to doing everything automatically online. There is also a big jump in technical complexity. Full e-commerce requires an understanding of how to run an online application for anyone on the web, keeping your server running, handling your own databases of stocks and orders, handling payments, monitoring shipments, etc. There are a number of application service providers (ASPs – see page 189) who can simplify this, but often full e-commerce is unnecessary.

One small religious charity we advised wished to sell books online. Given the likely scale of sales we pointed out that a relationship programme with a large online bookseller would give its potential customers all the service they could expect from the charity while providing similar income levels at much less technical and commercial risk. All the charity had to do was to add referral links to its site. For another small not-for-profit organisation, we pointed out the possibility of selling some of its used furniture via a recycling site. A complete discussion of e-commerce is beyond this chapter, but there is a tremendous amount of information available on the web using search tools.

E-procurement

E-procurement is the use of the internet for purchasing. Having obtained internet access, many not-for-profit organisations ignore some quick gains to be made by using it for purchasing. There are a number of ways of categorising online markets. One categorisation is:

- Direct sale – here's what we have.
- Catalogue sale – similar to mail order, here's our product line, but in addition you can order modifications, check delivery times, etc.
- Requisition order – similar to electronic data interchange (EDI): a complex order, perhaps with technical drawings or test specifications such as you might find within the automobile or aerospace industry.
- B2B exchange – similar to a stock exchange but for business goods, here's a place you can meet other buyers and sellers.

Between the buyers and sellers on the internet, there are a few distinctions worth mentioning:

- Many-to-one versus many-to-many – are many buyers acting in concert (e.g. reverse auctions) or is there a direct relationship of many buyers with a seller (e.g. stationery)?
- One-off versus relationship business – is there any advantage to repeat buying in a longer-term, structured relationship or is this simply a spot purchase based on cost or ready availability?
- Exchanges – typically these require active usage and management, probably only to be considered for important, regular purchases.

■ Re-intermediaries – the so-called new intermediaries on the internet who often perform important functions in helping buyers understand who the best sellers are at any moment, and helping sellers understand what is driving customers to them, information sellers often lose in direct sales. Re-intermediaries arise in many markets. In B2C good examples are helping people understand ways of investing (www.motley-fool.com) or helping people to find the best mortgage (www.charcolonline.co.uk). In B2B things are more complex but there are re-intermediaries for professional IT buyers (www.itnetwork.com) and many other subjects such as car fleets, telecommunications, oil and surplus goods.

Again, as in many things on the internet, reading is a poor substitute for exploration. For many small not-for-profit organisations, the benefits of e-procurement are not just more competitive prices. For instance, paperwork can be reduced, costs can be benchmarked, deliveries can be tracked. A simple example is stationery. Many online stationery providers permit even small users to set up budgets for categories of goods or their internal departments, develop a standard mini-catalogue of their own, provide for online secondary authorisation, obtain very detailed statistics on purchases, track deliveries, establish re-order limits and achieve bulk discounts over time. The only technical knowledge needed for supplier-supported e-procurement is how to use a web browser. Stationery and IT purchases are, at the time of writing, the two biggest B2B categories. It's easy to get started, because the supplier is doing all the hard work. It can even be fun.

For your not-for-profit organisations, another simple test is to look at your web site from the point of view of a prospective supplier:

■ Do you provide a list of common purchases and some idea of quantity (are you worth selling to)?
■ Do you indicate some of the principal budget holders for furniture, IT, stationery, transport or whatever, who buy in reasonable quantities (can I get in touch with the right person)?
■ Do you provide some breakdown of expenditure (not just for the financially curious, but also to help me understand if forms of outsourcing might help you)?

Not-for-profit organisations can also publish statements of their policies (e.g. opposition to child labour, environmental requirements, equal opportunities), procedures for registering suppliers or application forms for prospective suppliers. None of this requires technical work, simply web publishing.

For large not-for-profit organisations, e-procurement can be more complex. Linking an enterprise resource planning (ERP) package to dynamic purchase ordering, good receipt, stocks, and so on through to invoicing is quite tricky. Few large companies have sorted this out, let alone not-for-profit organisations. It is likely that some of the larger not-for-profit organisations, particularly those operating internationally, could use automated procurement systems for large or important purchases in a few categories, perhaps furniture, air travel, computers or healthcare. Not-for-profit organisations are so diverse it is hard to provide standard recommendations.

Application service providers

The high costs and complexity of IT have led some suppliers to provide common services to a range of organisations. Over the years, these suppliers have had various descriptions: computer bureaux, facilities management suppliers or outsourcers. Some fine distinctions have been made in this lineage (e.g. whether the clients own the computers which facilities managers run), but the basic premise is the same – sharing your IT needs with other users. The internet has added a new description, application service provider (ASP).

In some ways ASPs are more exciting than outsourcers. The common browser interface and the simplicity of inter-connection enable ASPs to provide specific services. Contrast this with an outsourcer who, in order to have a commercial proposition, would typically need a large chunk of computing to manage, e.g. all the desktops, or all the servers and applications, or the entire network (see chapter 19). ASPs are available for a variety of tasks:

- E-mail – many free e-mail services operate across the web (www.visto.com or www.hotmail.com). Anyone can connect to their e-mail anywhere they find a web browser with internet access. Small not-for-profit organisations often start providing e-mail by encouraging staff to use these services – no server, e-mail software or postbox is needed, there is integral virus control and global access. Some medium-sized and larger not-for-profit organisations are encouraging staff to use these e-mail services for personal e-mail so that work and personal affairs are not confused.
- Advertising – although web advertising is not very lucrative unless you have a lot of traffic, you can register your site with companies who will sell space on your web site for you (you have to insert some html which permits them to insert an advertisement).
- Site tracking – software to provide statistics on your web site usage can come from you (if you are hosting your web site

directly) or possibly from your internet service provider (ISP). You can also use site tracking ASPs (e.g. www.sitetracker.com).

- Finance – although at an early stage, many financial systems providers are providing pay-as-you-use software over the internet. A not-for-profit organisation can utilise an 'industrial strength' accounting system without running its own network or developing its software. Some specific finance functions, such as time-recording (e.g. www.timeserv.com), are also being provided by specialists. Why select a time-recording system, customise it, train your people and run the application when you can purchase it on the net and work nationally in groups on projects?.

- E-commerce – given the potential complexity of creating a full e-commerce site, it is not surprising to find ASPs offering to do most of the work. Some full service sites (e.g. www.shopcreator.com) provide catalogue support, account management, customer chat rooms, shopping trolleys, payment handling, e-mail confirmation, billing and sometimes even delivery and fulfilment. Better ASPs are often expensive, but sensible use by a small not-for-profit organisation can mean that the organisation simply needs e-mail connectivity to the ASP to offer 'customers' a high-quality web-shopping experience.

ASP examples are legion – financial modelling, web site construction, search engines, data storage and backup, wireless connections, online research, translation software or online diaries. There are even some emerging ASPs which permit unused home computer time to be co-ordinated for advanced research in bioinformatics (folding@home) or the search for extra-terrestrial intelligence (SETI@home). These projects are, of course, large-scale not-for-profit volunteering activities. Anything that can be delivered across the net is a potential ASP service. Many small organisations are building entire web-delivery capability with nothing more than access to a personal computer and a dial-up line to the internet.

While ASPs are an exciting development, they have many different commercial objectives. Some are trying to build pay-as-you-go services, some are based on the internet 'shareware ethos', some are still trying to make money on advertising or research from their users, while many others are free in the early stages but hope to charge later. Assume you won't get something for nothing, at least in the long-term. Most not-for-profit organisations should consider how using an ASP will help them (and also how their business will help the ASP) before designing their web strategy around one. ASPs are certainly useful at the fringe, for instance trying out an advanced search capability on your site

CASE EXAMPLE   The great smell of ASPs

One extreme example is a small cosmetics firm we know who outsources everything. The chief executive began by designing some insect-repellent scents and outsourced production of the scents and cosmetics to larger firms. She then used her husband's PC to use an ASP for building and hosting a free web site. Having built the web site, she used connections to other ASPs for site tracking, shopping trolleys, ordering and billing. Finally, she outsourced her warehousing and shipping to a firm which receives its instructions by e-mail from her billing ASP. She spends most of her time on traditional PR and promotion while the automated parts of the business are provided by others.

before purchasing a search engine. ASPs can be useful for the savvy user who is prepared to continue to put in work keeping up with the latest offerings. After all, most ASPs are invisible to your site visitor, so changing ASP from time to time shouldn't be too noticeable.

As with e-verything else, ASPs are evolving so rapidly that the best advice is to use the web to do your research (try starting with www.aspnews.com).

E-magination

To conclude this chapter, a few random ideas to jolt the imagination. Too often not-for-profit organisations believe that technical complexity prevents them from having imaginative sites. One of the earlier, creative uses of the web was Friends of the Earth's polluter databases and maps (www.foe.co.uk). This was simple and effective. If you are a small not-for-profit organisation with interesting information to hand, web publishing/searching/mapping it is not too difficult. Getting started with a web developer or programmer can often be kept within reasonable bounds to try out an idea. From there, popularity can determine whether future benefits exceed further development costs. Consider linking popular books around your cause to online bookstores. Consider posting form letters for sending to the appropriate politicians. Ensure you have a 'popular links' page out from your site. Extract key news stories about your cause for referencing. Consider using chat rooms for donors and beneficiaries. Allow people to register for e-mail newsletters. Provide calculators for environmental damage costs or benefits owed. Allow activists to register and manage fundraising projects online. Help people support beneficiaries with letters or 'adopt' an issue. Contemplate doing anything you do today on the internet. Imagine solving your most intractable problem through creative use of the web, then perhaps help other not-for-profit organisations to solve it through your own ASP!

Summary

- There is a sense of e-xpectation that the electronic world will increase in importance to not-for-profit organisations of all sizes.
- Consider possible uses of e-commerce (selling) and e-procurement (buying) for your not-for-profit organisation.
- Canny use of application service providers (ASPs) can help smaller not-for-profit organisations to get moving with e-commerce and e-procurement.
- Use your e-magination, the world of IT might create all manner of opportunities for your not-for-profit organisation.

Part 6

Case studies

Case studies – using this part

This part contains four detailed case studies, which look at each organisation or initiative in terms of the strategy, structure, systems etc. model used throughout the book. At the end of each case study, we set out lessons learned for other not-for-profit organisations. We believe that these case studies should be useful and interesting to most readers. Indeed, we'd like to take this opportunity to repeat our introductory plea to readers to come forward with interesting case studies for the second edition of this book. Please contact the authors by e-mail at hub@zyen.com or through our web site www.zyen.com if you wish to volunteer your (or another) organisation for a case study.

This part also contains an epilogue in which we revisit the themes set out in chapter 1and encourage the reader to learn to love IT.

Case studies

CASE STUDY City Parochial Foundation

IT strategy

City Parochial Foundation is a grant-making organisation based in the City of London. It has about fourteen staff and makes approximately 400 to 500 fresh awards and around 3000 to 4000 grant payments each year. City Parochial first embraced computing around 1986 with a Unix-based system, primarily for word processing. It also took on some Apple Macs to try to reduce the out-of-house costs for its publications etc. Around 1990 it moved office and decided to change IT at the same time. It chose to go exclusively Apple Mac-based, primarily because its publications are core to its business, and publishing houses at that time tended to be exclusively Mac-based.

More recent arrivals, such as head of finance Carol Harrison (ex Children's Society) and clerk to the trustees (chief executive equivalent) Bharat Mehta (ex National Schizophrenia Fellowship) questioned this strategy. However, they found that the use of IT at City Parochial was fit for the purpose and popular with staff. After Carol's arrival, she set up an IT group, which consisted of the IT manager, the accounts assistant and herself. This group organised a refresh of IT equipment in May 1999, continuing the inherited strategy. 'Most staff here are not screaming for IT change', Carol says, although people appreciated the improvements from the upgrades. 'We're sort of a publishing house', says Bharat. 'We've kept pace with the funding world', he says, while quickly caveating 'although the funding world is moving slowly. One of our main constraints is that other agencies are not progressing in their use of IT as perhaps they should.'

The strategy continues to be one of 'keep it simple', which seems to work well for City Parochial. One person commented that 'IT people often need to come down from Mount Olympus', implying that we humans are capable of making IT deliver the goods without excessive technology and without impenetrable jargon. The current author agrees.

IT structure

The only PC in the organisation is the file server, which helps make the network of iMacs talk to one another, with the help of Category 5 cabling, carrying voice and data, 100 Mbit Ethernet and TCP/IP protocols. The May 1999 refresh eliminated the one or two

'Year 2000 jitters' City Parochial had. Printing is networked and staff take a co-operative approach to it.

Aspirations include portable computers and projectors for the field staff, if budgets and needs permit/demand.

IT systems

Office tool kits are mostly Mac-based versions of Microsoft Word and Excel, although some users still use Macwrite Pro. The accounting system is Astra Premier, one of a few Mac-based accounting systems suitable for organisations of City Parochial's size and scale. Carol, who previously used CMG Fact 2000 and more latterly Great Plains Dynamics, describes the accounting system as 'basic but adequate. It interacts with Excel, so I can manipulate data for reports as much as I need to'.

City Parochial's grants database was developed in-house some ten years ago, using Filemaker Pro. It is basic, but again fit for purpose and well liked by the staff, including the newer arrivals. As Bharat points out, 'we do not use the current database to its full extent. We could extract more reports and interrogate the current system more'. The grants system is not integrated with the accounts system, but the amount of posting required between the two systems is small, so the users are not sure that integrating the two systems would 'pay back' adequately. (On cursory inspection, the current author concurred with the view that integration of the two systems is unlikely to be worth the effort at this time.)

Aspirations include trying out voice recognition software, which a few users have identified as having potential benefits.

IT staff, skills and style

The main IT person is Tina Stiff, who started as an administrator in 1984 and 'acquired the role of IT support after showing some ability to sort out printing on the Macs'. Tina shows great enthusiasm and composure when describing her work. She has good moral support and additional skills input from Bharat, Carol and others. She can cope with most issues that arise herself, only very occasionally needing to call on third parties for additional help on an ad hoc basis. City Parochial has chosen not to have maintenance contracts on machines, but to pay for repairs or buy replacements when necessary (it rarely is).

City Parochial outsources some of its functions, such as investment management and estates management, but has been relentless in its use of in-house resources for IT. This approach seems to have worked well for City Parochial for many years. Readers should note that City Parochial has been unusual in having for so many years the continuity of in-house IT skills which Tina brings.

IT shared values

Without burrowing deeply into City Parochial's data protection, security and safety environment, the set up came across as efficient, competent and safe. City Parochial aspires to progress quickly with external e-mail, a web site etc., which (at the time of writing) it had only recently started to explore. The trustees have accepted this need and are now keen for City Parochial to develop these aspects. This development will test City Parochial's self-sufficiency, especially in the data protection and information security areas. City Parochial is also keen to support other agencies to progress in the sensible use of IT; for example it is currently providing financial support for a funder/finder database CD-ROM project.

Lessons for other not-for-profit organisations

■ It is possible to be reasonably self-sufficient and have an impressive IT set up.

- Focusing on running core systems well can enable not-for-profit organisations to develop into new areas of IT activity from a position of strength.

- It helps to have continuity of (competent) staff to maintain a stable IT platform.
- It is possible to run a not-for-profit organisation using Apple Macs.

CASE STUDY BEN

IT strategy

BEN is the occupational benevolent fund for employees past and present (and their dependants) from the motor cycle, commercial vehicle and associated trades. BEN's mission is 'to help the strong in our industries to care for colleagues and dependants in time of need'. BEN achieves this mainly through running care homes and day centres, and by providing grants and loans to eligible people in need.

BEN might be seen as a reasonably typical medium-sized not-for-profit organisation. It has about forty IT users at its headquarters in Ascot, plus a further thirty or so spread amongst regional offices, care centres and home workers. BEN's IT strategy, formulated with Z/Yen in 1998, hinged on improving sharing information between its disparate systems and becoming increasingly self sufficient.

IT structure

BEN's IT structure is based around Hewlett Packard fileservers and Windows NT4 as the network operating system at headquarters. PCs are reasonably standard throughout the organisation, following a programme of upgrading and replacing machines, together with a rationalisation of IT support, in 1999.

At the time of writing, BEN is planning on expanding its network to encompass regional sites and care centres, using Citrix Metaframe to enable wide area networking for applications and Windows NT Remote Access Services to enable e-mail and internet access. The extent and speed at which this expansion occurs will be determined in part

by budget constraints and the cost/benefit balance of each element of that expansion. As many not-for-profit organisations find, the capital cost of this type of expansion is only part of the story – the ongoing costs of maintenance and line charges are a significant consideration for cash-strapped not-for-profit organisations like BEN.

IT systems

BEN has standardised on Microsoft Windows 95 and Office 97 as its basic systems tool kit. It uses SunAccount for its finances, APS for payroll, Raiser's Edge for fundraising, Coldharbour for residential care administration and Visual Alms for grant making (the latter system having been selected in 1999 and implemented in 1999/2000). BEN, unusually, runs a payroll-giving agency, for which it has a bespoke system based on Retrieve 4GL. This system, which was built by BEN's in-house IT person in the mid 1990s, was carefully checked for Year 2000 compliance and is now supported by Retrieve 4GL experts, Uniq systems.

In order to improve information sharing, BEN is working on devising common coding structures between systems, rather than fully-blown electronic integration. This approach will enable BEN to pull information together from disparate systems. For example it is keen to be able to tell a motor manufacturer how much money it has donated and how much has been contributed by its staff through payroll giving. Also, how much care has been provided and how much money has been given out in grants and loans to that same manufacturer's employees, former employees and their dependants, etc.

IT staff, skills and style

BEN has worked hard to use self-help where possible. IT support contracts are in place for the networks, machines and systems applications. However, BEN has moved away from the model of having a full-time in-house IT person, which it used for several years until just before its 1998 IT review. Subsequently, it has moved successfully to a model based on in-house 'owner/supporters' for major systems, 'superusers' to help support users of the office tool kits and several part-time network administrators to manage the day-to-day use of the network. BEN tends to use Z/Yen sporadically for specific projects and on a low-usage basis to help oversee the new model. This way of working has significantly reduced ongoing costs for BEN and improved the quality of its IT provision. BEN was keen to embrace the self-help model, which is not a universal style in the not-for-profit sector.

IT shared values

Because of its occupational links, BEN has been able to find help in some areas of its expansion, for example its neat and efficient web site which was designed and is supported by Motortrak (check out www.ben.org.uk). Nevertheless, BEN has had to grapple with the issues most not-for-profit organisations face, which is to realise that the management of the web site content is BEN's problem, not Motortrak's, and is probably the larger task. BEN is not overly ambitious in its use of IT, but has progressed considerably in past two to three years despite significant budget constraints.

Lessons for other not-for-profit organisations

- It is possible to move from a 'largely managed' to a 'largely self-help' model if you try.
- You need a lucky break to persevere with a bespoke system after its developer withdraws support.
- Standardising PCs reduces ongoing support and maintenance costs.
- Common coding structures are a good alternative to full-blown integration to start information sharing between fundraising and service provision systems, but you still need to do the hard thinking.

CASE STUDY   The Children's Society MART (co-author Nigel Hinks)

Strategy

The Children's Society (the Society) is committed to tackling the root causes of problems faced by children and young people, especially those whose circumstances make them particularly vulnerable. It has an annual income of about £40 million. The Society runs about 100 social work projects for children and young people. It employs around 1200 full-time equivalent staff.

The Social Work Performance Measurement and Recording Initiative (MART Initiative) was designed to equip social work projects and units with the knowledge and ability to undertake performance measurement and recording in a harmonised way. The benefits sought from the Initiative, originally set out in July 1998, are aligned with the Society's corporate plan. Those include encouraging good practice, improving the quality of information, evaluating the effectiveness of practice and providing the ability to measure and learn from information shared between groups of projects and units.

Structure

The IT structure required for this initiative was very straightforward. The Society already had established PCs in each project with Microsoft Office (including Access) available, together with modem links into a remote access e-mail service through headquarters. In a few larger projects, the Society has needed to implement small peer-to-peer networks to enable project workers to use MART efficiently and effectively. However, in the most part this initiative 'piggy-backed' on existing IT infrastructure, enabling the Initiative team to concentrate its attention on the specific tools and methodologies needed to see through the initiative vision.

Systems

The objectives and benefits are focused on skills more than tools. However, the Society, in its corporate plan, sought to 'develop the necessary internal tools to align the organisation to our external aims'. The tools designed to support the Initiative are:

- **MART**: the Measurement and Recording Template, which has been developed over the past year by the Society's IT department specifically to support this work. MART is a configurable Microsoft Access database, which provides a common data structure while enabling projects/units to meet local information needs safely, securely and flexibly.
- **SMART**: Several 'MARTs', allowing data from several MART sites to be consolidated for reporting, comparison and shared learning. SMART should help the social work and other divisions (e.g. fundraising, communications, finance).

The Society used a 'stage gate' or phased approach, to reduce uncertainty through relatively short phases of work until the concepts and tools were proven. At the end of the first 'proof of concept phase', working with three projects, the Society defined nine key benefits for the initiative, against all of which qualitative and quantitative measures could be set and evaluated. Technical developments were run as separate phases of work. At the end of each phase, the Society

devised a project plan for the next phase. An Initiative Board provided management for the MART Initiative; the Social Work Divisional Management Team provided governance, signing off each key phase. At the end of the pilot, the Society undertook a comprehensive evaluation of the MART Initiative.

The IT development was a fairly low-key matter, with one Society Access expert working part-time on the initiative for about eighteen months, under the supervision of Z/Yen. In the later stages, other Society staff were involved in the testing and brainstorming on improvements to the tool. The emphasis from the outset was on skills transfer to ensure that the Society would be self-sufficient once the initiative was implemented.

Staff, skills and style

The pilot was undertaken and evaluated in collaboration with Z/Yen. The process of engagement between the Initiative Team and individual projects/units involved ten to twelve days of direct contact over a three to four month period. The process involved:

- **Planning**: prioritisation, resource allocation and communication. The methodology has a checklist to help plan a viable implementation strategy at each site.
- **Design**: direct work with local teams to analyse information needs, using workshops, iterative preparation and agreement of data capture sheets, 'building' a local version of MART.
- **Implementation**: installing MART, materials and initial training, starting capturing data, top up training and support, sometimes working in groups with other projects/units.
- **Review**: through telephone and visits to help the project/unit progress and to evaluate the achievement of each project/unit's benefits.

These results have been very encouraging, enabling the Society to proceed with full-scale rollout to projects and units across the country. The feedback from pilot participants has enabled the Society further to improve the MART Initiative for the rollout. The Society has now built a team of four facilitator/implementers who travel the country helping individual projects to implement the Initiative.

The collaborative nature of the MART Initiative (between the Society's Social Work Division, its IT department, its projects/units and Z/Yen) has maintained an environment of co-operation, ideas generation and continuous improvement. It is a model example of inter-departmental and inter-organisation co-operation achieving excellent results.

The enthusiasm for the MART Initiative within most projects and units involved has been refreshing. People in projects especially like the skills transfer, which enables them to learn to look after themselves. They also like the fact that some benefits flow early (e.g. the information needs stage gets people to challenge the way that they do things, often leading to quick, indirect benefits from the MART Initiative).

Shared values

The knowledge learned from the pilot is being used throughout the rollout to over 120 projects and units from 2000 to 2002. The Society is already using knowledge obtained through this Initiative on other Society initiatives (e.g. planning and project

management of IT projects, information models used for liaison between departments, MART potentially being used as a tool in other Society departments). The Society is already liaising with other similar organisations (e.g. Barnardo's), starting to share the learning and intending to publish appropriate papers on the Initiative to benefit the charity sector as a whole. The methods, tools and lessons learned should be readily adaptable to benefit almost any charity involved with service provision – large or small.

Lessons for other not-for-profit organisations

- Most Children's Society sites are quite small, so the model shown in the case study is valid for individual, small operational not-for-profits or collections of small project-based activities.
- The database tool is far less important than the thinking the projects do about their work flows, recording requirements and information needs.
- When taking on ambitious projects the stage gate approach – i.e. to pilot, prototype, test, then roll-out – minimises risk (you can bail out early) and maximises the chances of success (you can refine and improve as you go).
- Trickling down skills (e.g. using third parties to train your key people who then train the rest of your people) can keep costs down to manageable levels and encourage ownership of the initiative.

CASE STUDY Youthnet

IT strategy

Youthnet began as a spin-off idea from the 1995 hit book *Go For It* by Martin Lewis. The book was a directory interspersed with inspirational writings to encourage young people to get involved in 'good things'. The

initial idea was simple enough; the information contained in *Go For It* should be available on a web site. This idea was a little ahead of its time but practicable in 1995/96. A small team used minimal technology to replicate the book's content on a web site as quickly and easily as possible. Anastasia Williams, chief executive of Youthnet at the time, reckons that the first version cost about £200. 'We used shovelware', she boasts, 'the simplest tools to shovel the data onto the web as quickly and easily as possible'.

The team immediately started planning the next version, with which it aspired to achieve a lot more and which it knew would need a lot more resources. Its strategy was to be an updateable resource on the web. The resource would be robust, would be able to utilise electronic information from other not-for-profit and statutory sources and would need minimal intervention and rekeying to maintain. 'Shovelware' would no longer do. Version 2 cost about £500,000, which Youthnet managed to beg and/or borrow – about £200,000 in cash and the rest as gifts in kind. The site was launched in February 1997 and quickly started to win awards. Anastasia describes the site as being 'a bit like a dishwasher. As soon as people started to use it they couldn't work out how they had managed without it before'. But there were gaps, particularly in the scope of the information services available, and the feeds from other information services were far from the self-maintaining vision.

Youthnet promptly started planning Version 3 to put many of those matters right. By this time Youthnet was starting to employ its own core team and was becoming increasingly able to look after itself. A key benefit for Version 3 was a simple database feeder system for members of the volunteer bureau network (and others) to use. Version 3 cost more, probably about £1.2 million. The Prime Minister, Tony Blair, launched the site in May 2000.

The team is already formulating plans for Version 4, aiming for yet more self-maintenance within the system and increasingly seeking real time links, which are vital for some forms of information (e.g. current availability of hostel places on any

particular night). Youthnet has spun off the web site, www.thesite.org, as a trading subsidiary, with Anastasia as chief executive. This should enable the site to continue to develop but along more commercial lines, while Youthnet concentrates on ensuring that its charitable objectives are being furthered.

IT structure

The internal systems are quite straight-forward; a small PC network using Sun Microsystems servers as the web servers. Again, Youthnet went for industry standards and managed to get generous donations of the desired equipment at first. Such generosity is rare from major suppliers, but the innovation and high profile of this particular project will have helped Youthnet to get started down this path with appropriate, donated kit.

IT systems

The underlying databases are based on Oracle and Vbase. Anastasia described Version 2 as 'a cheap armour plated version to see through the new vision'. For that reason, Youthnet wanted to use industry standard tools for the core databases. Oracle generously donated licences, probably because the project was especially innovative and high profile. Youthnet needed simple feeder databases at low/no cost for impecunious user organisations, such as members of the volunteer bureau network. Fiona Dawe, now chief executive of Youthnet and former head of the National Centre for Volunteering, explained why the self-maintaining databases idea was so important. 'People are willing to fund and sponsor the creative work far more readily than the ongoing maintenance. We needed to minimise the ongoing information maintenance costs to ensure survival beyond the initial burst phases.'

Anastasia summarises the approach used over the several versions as 'pilot cheap, then do it well'. The current author commends this approach for innovative IT projects as a key way to minimise risks and maximise rewards.

IT staff, skills and style

Youthnet's approach to staff and skills varied considerably through the versions of the project. Version 1, the 'shovelware' version, was minimal; Youthnet essentially did it in-house with borrowed help. Youthnet relied heavily on third party help for Version 2, provided in this case mainly by Web Media for the web design and Media Surface for the database integration. By the time Version 3 was being built, Youthnet had started to build its own team sufficiently to take on most of the work in-house again, using a mixture of core staff and freelancers. This is broadly its staff and skills position today. Under the new structure, Youthnet employs about nine people, of whom one is deemed to be the in-house IT person. The trading subsidiary — thesite.org — employs six people, two of whom might be described as technical people and two as web content specialists.

Youthnet's style is clearly entrepreneurial, youthful and 'can-do' in ways not regularly seen in the not-for-profit sector. Despite this, Youthnet seems to have spotted early that robustness and systems safety were going to be key to thesite.org's ongoing success.

IT shared values

By the start of 1998 (less than one year in to Version 2), thesite.org had some 12,000 records and was growing at 1000 records a month. Contrast this with the total of 400 or so records contained in Version 1. Youthnet grappled early with data protection issues and (probably more pertinently) copyright issues. As the number, diversity and immediacy of feeds grows, Youthnet will find these issues increasingly important.

Lessons for other not-for-profit organisations

- You can have entrepreneurial-style not-for-profit organisations.
- Internet-based technologies are very suitable for information resource provision projects and initiatives.
- Start modest and then build from there.
- Don't be afraid to switch between outsourced and in-house provision of IT services if/when your circumstances change accordingly.

Epilogue

How to stop worrying and learn to love IT

Themes revisited

Risk/reward management is the slightly scientific art of minimising risks and maximising rewards for an organisation. The techniques, encompassed by the Z/Ealous methodology sketched out in chapter 1, help organisations to manage uncertainty. We argue that IT management contains such uncertainty and therefore lends itself well to risk/reward management. This book seeks to help not-for-profit organisations to minimise the risks and maximise the rewards they get from using IT. The other themes we set out in the introduction can be seen as means to that end:

- Prioritising your planned use of IT.
- Agreeing objectives and scope.
- Using proper processes for choosing solutions.
- Communication, contribution, consensus, commitment (the four Cs).

Whatever aspect of your IT you are looking at, these principles apply, be it a refresh of equipment, a change of a core system, organising your human resources to manage your IT or your latest internet-based initiative. Similarly, the mantra 'plan, implement, evaluate' pervades any IT project or initiative you are attempting. Well-planned IT projects are less risky and more likely to yield the desired rewards. Implement your IT projects in manageable, bite-sized chunks. Do evaluate your projects, learning from the good and the bad, to help you minimise the risks and maximise the rewards.

Why worry?

IT can help not-for-profit organisations to:

- Waste less money on uneconomic and/or inefficient work practices.
- Apply more resources directly towards their beneficiaries.
- Apply those resources more effectively towards their organisation's objectives (e.g. charitable purposes).
- Better inform their stakeholders and beneficiaries.

Yet to many not-for-profit sector people IT remains a source of worry. Indeed many have confided in us that the IT area worries them more than any other aspect of their work. Perhaps this is because in many not-for-profit organisations responsibility for IT rests with an individual who knows little about IT. Perhaps it is because in the not-for-profit sector it can be difficult to justify the significant IT spending using straightforward cost/benefit analysis. Perhaps the worry is inevitable, caused by inherent technophobia and technoscepticism.

Putting it another way, the not-for-profit sector manager, perhaps as a result of responsibilities or perhaps as a result of inherent perception of the uncertainties involved in choosing and using IT, tends to make non-optimal risk-based decisions. Symptoms of the potential for such non-optimal decisions might be:

- Inappropriate, very low or non-existent spend on IT.
- 'Pendulum-swing' decision making – which might be inappropriately low spend on IT followed by inappropriately high spend on one system or initiative.
- Protracted selection processes that never quite conclude.
- Snap decisions on choosing major items which cannot possibly have taken into account sufficient research and information.
- Blame and shame investigations into any aspect of an IT project which might not have gone exactly right.
- Refusal to allow post-implementation evaluation of IT projects.

Don't worry, be happy

Contrast the above mood of worry with the easy attitude of many young people, who seem able to enjoy IT and benefit from it almost effortlessly. Of course, those young people do not carry on their shoulders the responsibility for managing an organisation, nor do they have to justify whether the spending is in the interests of beneficiaries and stakeholders. However, perhaps there is a more profound psychological difference, based on the willingness to accept inherent uncertainty and a willingness to experiment and 'fail' as long as the downside of failure is not too profound.

We suggest that many young people tend to accept and embrace new worlds without worrying too much about whether they understand them to the full. This 'go with the flow' attitude can be observed in young people's attitudes towards other areas. For example observe their easy acceptance of other worlds such as Star Wars – a futuristic new technology world – and Harry Potter – a magical 'old world', full of wizards (humans with magical powers) and muggles (humans who do not recognise magic even when it confronts them).

The IT arena is a fast changing and sometimes confusing place, but we do not need to understand all the technology and wizardry IT entails to be able to benefit from it. Indeed, many of the most effective stories shown in the case studies in this book have been the result of experimentation into the unknown, but done in a controlled way that did not jeopardise the organisation.

We hope that this book will benefit readers, by which we mean (at least in part) to help them stop worrying and enjoy the benefits of IT. Go with the flow. In the same way as we advocate evaluation for continuous improvement of IT systems, we welcome your evaluation of this book to help us to improve future editions. Please let us know.

Summary

- Define the benefits your charity can gain from IT.
- Drive through those benefits using risk/reward management to minimise the risks and maximise the rewards.
- Enjoy the benefits of IT.
- Stop worrying.
- Experiment in a controlled way.
- Go with the flow.
- May the force be with you.
- Don't be a muggle.

Appendix A
Technology horizons

Smaller, faster, cheaper

As a reader of this book you deserve the authors' best guess at some of the future technologies which might be of importance to the not-for-profit sector. We shall go out on a long limb and share with you some trends which we believe have some staying power and are worth bearing in mind when formulating an IT strategy for a not-for-profit organisation.

Before we start on some the wacky or esoteric technologies we should encourage you to experiment where possible if you want to investigate new technologies. Such experimentation is often within the means of not-for-profit organisations. For instance, have you tried:

- Personal digital assistants (say a Palm or Psion).
- Speech recognition software.
- A barcode scanner.
- A digital camera.
- A text scanner.
- A pet robot.
- A WAP phone.
- Any other new or strange device?

Why not? Many of these 'toys' can teach you a lot about the current or future limits of computing devices and at much less cost than a conference or a consultant.

New devices, new software and new technologies come out constantly. Good sources of product announcements are the COMDEX exhibitions in the USA. Other sources include a variety of e-magazines on the web. On the other hand, technology doesn't really change all that rapidly. Most of the technologies today had some prototype in the 1960s or 1970s – for instance, pull-down menus, mice, foldable computers, wearable computers, pliable computers, 35mm slide machines, scanners, 3D holographic imaging, handheld computers, voice recognition. The internet existed by 1970 (one of the authors was using the internet in 1976). Announcements of the twenty-first century may not be novel but they do tend to be 'smaller, faster, cheaper'. This puts technology that seemed futuristic a few years ago within the means of even smaller not-for-profit organisations today.

In short, the remarkable thing today is not new technology, but the ubiquity of computers and networks because they are more portable, much less expensive and do so much more. At least as interesting are the complex dynamics and timing of technology take-up. Why did the internet not become a popular commercial and consumer tool until the late 1990s? Why did the personal computer succeed without networks and with limited storage and processor speed? The late night conversations on these subjects haven't yet reached consensus, and there are many more similar questions. What is clear is that just because a great technology exists doesn't mean it will be successful. Likewise, just because something is successful doesn't mean it is a great technology. Technology adoption appears to be inherently complex and bears more than a passing resemblance to fad and fashion. Not-for-profit organisations should be careful not to spend money 'riding a possible fad wave'. Conversely, they should not be so slow to adopt technologies that they miss out on possible benefits for years.

E-nduring themes

Amidst all this confusion, we believe that there are four enduring themes which are useful to keep in mind alongside 'smaller, cheaper, faster' when contemplating the likely future of technologies for the not-for-profit sector. These themes seem to underlie much past development:

- *Ever-widening world:* in which computers have moved out from laboratories to companies to hobbyists to homes to devices to phone networks and have become more and more interconnected.
- *IT as a utility:* in which people rapidly take for granted yesterday's exciting technology and by tomorrow will demand, even insist, that it perform flawlessly.
- *Relationship management:* time and again the winners of commercial technology battles seem to be those who service client relationships successfully, not those with the best technology.
- *Human-machine interface advances:* the biggest technology jumps are most evident in the interfaces between people and machines.

Ever-widening world

This world is one in which computers and networks are ubiquitous. Not just a computer and internet connection in every home and office, but computers driving every appliance, every light bulb having an internet connection, computer-controlled bodily functions, injectible computers, neuron altering computers or computerised plants using photoluminescence to light footpaths. In many ways this world is frightening. One of the obvious social consequences is a lack of privacy and a heightened awareness of security. Indeed some not-for-profit human rights organisations are turning their attention to these issues from a campaigning perspective (e.g. campaigning against lack of privacy).

People are more and more aware of their increasing vulnerability. Your every move can be tracked, if not by satellite then by credit card transactions, by CCTV, by digital car registration readers, by travel card, by mobile phone, by internet connection, by telephone call, etc. Some of the things to look out for socially are intense debates on privacy, data ownership, data use and identity cards with many possible backlashes against the technophilia. As a not-for-profit organisation, the home management systems and increasing information can permit some interesting advances, e.g. better automated care in the home, patient-oriented epidemiological studies, improved emergency responses, pre-identification of troublesome issues or better activist deployment.

Two of the more interesting new technologies are wireless applications protocol (WAP) and Bluetooth. WAP is basically the ability to connect to the internet or internet-style services over a mobile phone. Bluetooth is a standard supported by a large number of consumer-device suppliers to permit all devices to communicate with each other easily using small, local networks constructed on-the-fly, for instance your mobile phone chatting to your Palm device talking to your office computer to update new addresses. Both of these technologies have the capability of increasing the pervasiveness of computing and networks. While these particular implementations of the technologies might not stand the test of time, and assuming costs come down to 'consumer price levels', not-for-profit organisations can envisage being able to utilise these types of tools amongst their activists, field workers and/or volunteers.

IT as a utility

The internet has already subverted some old information management techniques. If you have been working with the internet on demand for several years as the authors have (i.e. a cheap, rapid connection), you suddenly find that some old 'working methods' are not needed. Humour or joke books are unnecessary (reference sites and circulating e-mails flood you); searching for quotations is a doddle; the search engine is your encyclopaedia or you can directly access encyclopaedias online; if your hand-held dictionary or thesaurus is incomplete, better resources are online. At first it is a bit strange when a guest or child asks for an explanation to jump online and find it, but it soon becomes normal. These are just some simple examples of how IT is becoming a utility.

In the workplace we now find chief executives who arrive at their office and cannot start their day because the system is down and their automated diary is unavailable. Businesses find when their e-mail server is blocked that their productivity tumbles, their suppliers become confused, their clients get angry. But they didn't even use the term e-mail a few years ago. In many ways IT is becoming a utility for businesses and, a bit more slowly, homes. Services such as online diaries have gone from being a slightly useful toy to becoming 'mission critical'.

Some of the things to look out for include new commercial offerings which trade a bit of reduced functionality or leading-edge capability for a marked increase in reliability. Increasingly, customers demand 'five-nines' reliability, (99.999 per cent availability of service). Utility services already exist which provide off-site backup over the internet – hotstart backup sites, emergency e-mail changeover or automatic anti-virus configuration and set up. You can expect to see all manner of redundant service provision – high availability ISPs, satellite network connections or rent-a-computer. The ASP (application service provider) companies already provide IT as a utility in simple areas such as e-mail and diaries. They emphasise that their focus on service far surpasses the ability of most internal systems providers. 'Eliminate the amateurs, use the professionals.' You already see more focus on enforceable sanctions for poor service or insurance against some types of failures. Pay-as-you-go services can be helpful to impecunious not-for-profit organisations with limited capital budgets and/or uncertainty as to the growth in activity they expect. You might anticipate reduced costs and better services. We therefore predict that more not-for-profit organisations will be able to consider more comprehensive outsourcing of IT utilities as time goes on. We have already detected this trend starting in our professional work with larger not-for-profit organisations.

Relationship management

B2C (business to consumer) companies may be risky investments, but they have achieved much in a short time. B2C has proved that good customer service can be delivered online to demanding consumers. This rapid development of relationship management has fed back into companies where the end-users of corporate systems can see that some of their consumer information technology services far exceed their corporate ones. Customers – retail, corporate or even beneficiaries – are becoming more demanding. Organisations are responding, hence much of the current intensity surrounding customer relationship management (CRM) systems or citizen relationship management systems (also CRM). Expect to see beneficiary (BRM) and donor (DRM) parallels soon.

Human-machine interface advances

Direct interfaces with people are still advancing and have room for tremendous improvement – speech recognition is a key area affecting the future success of mobile phones, WAP and Bluetooth. There are still some new or early areas for interfaces such as holograms, smell, direct brain connections, wearable computers, internal computers and whole-body sensors. In some ways the human-machine interface needs its greatest improvement at the data analysis level. Floods of information are generating new statistical and computation techniques for handling very large datasets or transactions. Even more interesting is the move to handling imprecise information such as the probability of being right about the identity of a person. Expect to see much more emphasis on 3D visualisation of large data volumes – 3D images for health care and/or education, a financial landscape for your accounts or risk-based simulations of geo-political forces on environmental issues.

A difficult, practical information problem today is handling uncertainty both in data and in future projections. Ways of helping people deal with imprecise or difficult information include intelligent agents (for instance www.tryllian.com), neural networks, Bayesian engines or some of the new predictive hierarchical clustering approaches. These technologies might enable sophisticated counselling assistance, interactive training, information provision, electronic negotiation aides etc.

E-normous potential

We opened with 'smaller, cheaper, faster'. Human demands for processing power drive manufacturers to look at ways of increasing processing power markedly. Some direct advances are being made by organisations working on the enormous human proteome project, e.g. IBM's Blue Gene. Other interesting ideas include the use of spare computing time (most computers are idle most of the time) across large numbers of computers, e.g. SETI@home or folding@home. This is, after all, not-for-profit use of spare computer time. Can you envisage being able to persuade your supporters to donate computer time to support the computing needs of one of your not-for-profit organisation's activities? There is a great deal of interest in such peer to peer computing, which essentially enables individuals to work together using the internet as the medium. Peer to peer technology has also found consumer applications, such as Napster and Gnuttella, which help people to share intellectual property, such as music, across the web.

Finally, although probably several years off, quantum computers have the potential to become instantaneous super-computers at the sub-atomic level. Certainly smaller and infinitely faster, if not cheaper. The most fascinating aspect of quantum computers should be their ability to break through many traditional problems which could not be solved even on the fastest imaginable traditional computer. Many existing applications could use super-computers today (such as web site personalisation) but there are also many problems (such as the 'travelling fundraiser' problem – he or she needs to visit a certain number of cities, calculate the most efficient route) which are intractable when they hit real-world numbers. Examples include real-time multi-model logistics, multi-flight-scheduling, some complex auctions, dynamic pricing and portfolio balancing. While these applications might seem a long way away from your not-for-profit organisation's activities, many not-for-profits do grapple with analogous problems:

- Logistics (e.g. optimising meals on wheels deliveries).
- Multi-scheduling (e.g. care home rostering).
- Auctions (could you get more from those donated gifts with IT to help you run your charity auctions?).
- Dynamic pricing (charity mail order and/or shops).
- Portfolio balancing (maximising returns and minimising risk of your not-for-profit's investments).

Technology horizons in brief

Don't be afraid to try new technologies at the consumer level for fun – it can be a cost-effective way to experiment and learn. Many of the enduring trends in technology are likely to have significant, beneficial effects on the not-for-profit sector. Try to keep an eye on trends, so that once a technology that you fancy becomes small enough, fast enough and cheap enough for your organisation, you will be ready for it. It can help not-for-profit organisations to use the financial services sector as a 'crystal ball' for the sector – most technology that becomes ubiquitous in the trading room today will probably become ubiquitous in larger not-for-profit sector organisations within five years. Five years is within the business strategy horizon of most not-for-profit organisations.

Appendix B
Directory

Further reading

The following is a small sample of not-for-profit sector specific texts and one or two good general primers. Readers who are keen to pursue detailed further reading on any of the topics covered in this chapter are welcome to contact the authors for further sources.

Bazerman, M., 1998 *Judgement in Managerial Decision Making*, John Wiley and Sons (excellent treatise on decision making)

Berger, S., 1997 *How to Have a Meaningful Relationship With Your Computer*, Sunstar Publishing (light but useful read on coming to terms with your computer)

Burt, E. and Taylor, J., 1999 *Information and Communications Technology: Reshaping the Voluntary Sector in the Information Age?*, Centre for the Study of Telematics and Governance, Glasgow Caledonian University www.brunel.ac.uk/research/virtsoc/reports/voluntarymain.htm

Business Accounting Systems Year Book, ICAEW Faculty of Information Technology, November 1999 (information resource for software in various sector categories)

Callaghan, J., 1992 *Costing for Contracts*, Directory of Social Change (practical guidelines for charities negotiating contracts with outside suppliers)

Chapman, J., 2000 *Helpdesk Management*, Hodder and Stoughton (chapter and verse on managing an IT helpdesk)

Clegg et al., 1996 *The Performance of Information Technology and the Role of Human and Organisational Factors*, University of Sheffield www.system-concepts.com/stds/clegg/html#RTFToC3

Davis, S. and Meyer, C., 1998 *Blur*, Addison Wesley (more scare than flair, but worth a read if you like tracking trends)

English, E., 1995 *Computer*, Edittech International

Froehlich, T. *Fundraising Software 101* located at: www.tfraise.com/ frs101 (web site with overview of available fundraising software explaining how to evaluate and select the right system for your charity)

Gann, N., 1996 *Managing Change in Voluntary Organisations*, Open University Press, 1996 (covers not-for-profit sector change management generally, contains IT related examples)

Gookin, D., *PCs for Dummies*, IDG Books, regularly updated (useful 'how to' guidebooks and not really for dummies)

Hambridge, S., 1995 *Netiquette Guidelines, Responsible Use of the Network Working Group*, www.cybernothing.org/cno/docs/ rfc1855.html and many other web sites (good practice guidance on using shared systems)

Harris, I. and Mainelli, M., 1991 *Zitt*, Z/Yen Limited (informative IT trivia game)

Harris, I., Mainelli, M. and Smith, M., 1996 *Charities and the Internet*, Z/Yen Limited (demystifies the basics of the internet)

The Hutchinson Dictionary of Computing, Multi Media and the Internet, second edition, Helicon Publishing Limited, regularly updated (useful handbook of terms and concepts)

The Institute of Chartered Accountants of Scotland, 1999 *Controlling Computers in Business* – volumes 1 to 6, The Institute of Chartered Accountants of Scotland (useful texts on issues such as security, data protection, disaster recovery etc.)

Kibbe, B. and Setterberg, F., 1992 *Succeeding with Consultants: Self Assessment for the Changing Nonprofit*, The David and Lucille Packard Foundation (very US style but contains useful tips on using consultants)

Lake, H., 1996 *Direct Connections Guide to Fundraising on the Internet*, Aurelian Information Ltd (resource guide on fundraising using the internet)

Lanning, A., 1997 *Managing NonProfits on the Internet*, Aurelian Information Ltd (useful book with further ideas for internet-based work)

Lawrie, A., 1996 *The Complete Guide to Creating and Managing New Projects: for Charities and Voluntary Organisations*, Directory of Social Change (guidance on general project management for not-for-profit sector organisations)

Lessig, L., 1999 *Code and Other Laws of Cyberspace*, Basic Books (menacing text on the ethical issues raised by the internet)

Lumsden, G. and Lumsden, D., 1993 'Problem Solving with Information and Analysis', in *The Non Profit Management Handbook*, John Wiley and Sons (methodology for making decisions in not-for-profits)

Mainelli, M. and Harris, I., 2000 *Clean Business Cuisine*, Milet (only somewhat relevant – Gizmo's Big Adventure for example – but a thumping good read and a Sunday Times Book of the Week)

Pfaffenberger, B., *Computer User's Dictionary*, Que, regularly updated (another useful handbook of terms and concepts).

Rinaldi, A.H., 1998 *The Net: User Guidelines and Netiquette*, www.fau.edu/netiquette/net/index.html (more good practice on sharing systems)

Santayana, G., 1905-6 'Flux and Constancy in Human Nature', in *Life of Reason*, vol. 1, ch. xii

Shapiro, A.L., 1999 *The Control Revolution*, Century Foundation (high grade self confessed cyber punditry)

Shapiro, C. and Varian, H.R., 2000 *Information Rules*, Harvard Business School Press (excellent text on the principles of the information economy)

Shurkin, J., 1996 *Engines of the Mind*, Norton (interesting book on the evolution of technology)

Taffinder, P., 1998 *Big Change*, John Wiley and Sons (sound text on change management, rated '4.5 on the FDA Scale' by Ian Harris in *Strategy Magazine*, September 1999)

Taylor, A., 2001 www.bcs.org.uk/review/2001/html/po61.htm British Computer Society (study using Standish criteria for success)

Various authors, 1999 [tool kit software package e.g., Word, Excel, Access Lotus 123, etc] *for Dummies*, IDG Books (entertaining and jargon free series of books which should explain any office system and provide useful tips and techniques for working more effectively with it. They cover a vast array of subjects, including most major office tool kits and operating systems)

Vogel, S., 1997 *First Steps on the Internet for Business and the Voluntary Sector*, Aurelian Information Ltd (good starter book and suitable for smaller organisations who want to get started on the internet)

www.sutherla.dircon.co.uk/volunteer (a 1998 study of the development of the internet within the voluntary sector)

Useful addresses and sources of further information

Ask Jeeves Search Engine – askjeeves.com/ (useful search engine which responds to plain English queries and searches all the major search engines – Excite, Alta Vista, Yahoo etc. – for you)

Association of Charitable Foundations – www.acf.org.uk/ (web site with good list of publications and links to member organisations)

British Standards Institution (BSI) – 389 Chiswick High Road, London W4 4AL, tel 020 8996 7000, fax 020 8996 7001, www.bsi.org

Caritas Data – www.caritasdata.co.uk (an information service
for all those involved in the voluntary sector, with full
financial information on the top 500 charities, articles
and other links)

Charity Commissioners of England and Wales – www.charity-
commission.gov.uk/ (including links and full list of
publications)

Charity Net – www.charitynet.org (portal site for charities with
links, discussion area etc.)

Chartech – see Institute of Chartered Accountants in England and
Wales: IT Faculty

Claris – www.apple.com/appleworks/ (home page for the Claris
range of software)

Foundation Center – fdncenter.org/ (US site with long list of
publications and guides to managing your charity)

Fundraising UK – www.fundraising.co.uk (one of the first online
information services for fundraisers with news archives going
back to 1995 and a large bookshop)

Health and Safety Executive (HSE) – HSE Infoline 08701 545500,
open 8.30 am to 5 pm Monday to Friday, e-mail:
Public.enquiries@hse.gov

HTML tutorial – www.htmlgoodies.com (a friendly series of
tutorials in the basics of HTML programming, allowing you to
create your own web pages)

Institute of Charity Fundraising Managers – 208 Market Towers, Nine
Elms Lane, London SW8 5NQ, tel 020 7627 3436

Institute of Chartered Accountants in England and Wales: IT Faculty –
PO Box 433, Chartered Accountants Hall, Moorgate Place,
London EC2P 2BJ, tel 020 7920 8481, fax 020 7628 1791, e-mail:
itfac@icaew.co.uk www.itfac.co.uk

Institute of Chartered Accountants of Scotland – 27 Queen Street,
Edinburgh, EH2 1LA, tel 0131 247 4817, fax 0131 247 4828

Institute of Management Consultants – 5th Floor, 32-33 Hatton
Garden, London EC1N 8DL, tel 020 7242 2140, fax 020 7831
4597, e-mail: consult@imc.co.uk www.imc.co.uk/

The IT Resource Guide for UK Charities and Non-Profit Organisations –
www.itforcharities.co.uk/

Joseph Rowntree Foundation – www.jrf.org.uk/ (including reports
and useful links)

Linux – www.linux.org (contains more information on the Linux
operating system)

Lotus – www.lotus.com (home page for all Lotus products)

Microsoft – www.microsoft.com (home page for all Microsoft
products)

National Council of Voluntary Organisations – www.ncvo-vol.org.uk/
(includes a useful series of links to voluntary sector resources
on line)

Partnerships Online – www.partnerships.org.uk/ (guide to setting up virtual partnerships and communities)

PRINCE 2 – www.apmgroup.co.uk/p2index.htm (guide to PRINCE 2 project management methodology, including introduction, bibliography and sample product outlines)

Star Office – www.sun.com/staroffice/ (home page of Star Office; site to find out more about Star Office and download the software)

Technical Encyclopaedia – www.techweb.com/encyclopedia/ (easy to use encyclopaedia of technical and computing terms)

University of Wales, Lampeter – www.lampeter.ac.uk/pdu/www.html (useful listing of charity and voluntary sector links in the UK and Europe)

Voluntary Organisations Internet Server – www.vois.org.uk (VOIS hosts the web pages of many charities as well as providing a bulletin board service for volunteers)

Z/Yen Limited – 5-7 St Helen's Place, London EC3A 6AU, tel 020 7562 9562, fax 020 7628 5751, e-mail: hub@zyen.com, www.zyen.com

Index